ROBLOX
TOP ADVENTURE GAMES

HARPER

An Imprint of HarperCollinsPublishers

CONTENTS

TREELANDS 8-9

APOCALYPSE RISING 10-11

JAILBREAK 12-13

SHARK ATTACK! 14-15

NATURAL DISASTER SURVIVAL 16-17

INNOVATION LABS 18-19

ROBLOX DEATHRUN 20-21

MOON TYCOON 22-23

IMPERIUM 24-25

MOUNT OF THE GODS 26-27

NEVERLAND LAGOON 28-29

TRADELANDS 30-31

PRISON LIFE 32-33

TEMPLE OF MEMORIES 34-35

HEROES OF ROBLOXIA 36-37

WOLVES' LIFE 2 38-39

ZOMBIE RUSH 40-41

GALAXY 42-43

SHARD SEEKERS 44-45

ULTIMATE DRIVING: WESTOVER ISLANDS 46-47

WHATEVER FLOATS YOUR BOAT 48-49

AFTER THE FLASH: DEEP SIX 50-51

PINEWOOD COMPUTER CORE 52-53

MINER'S HAVEN 54-55

HIDE AND SEEK EXTREME 56-57

FLOOD ESCAPE 58-59

CAR CRUSHERS 60-61

FANTASTIC FRONTIER 62-63

ROBLOX TITANIC 64-65

MAD PAINTBALL 2 66-67

WORLD EXPEDITION 68-69

THE NORMAL ELEVATOR 70-71

MINING INC! 72-73

CLEANING SIMULATOR 74-75

LUMBER TYCOON 2 76-77

SKYBOUND 2 78-79

KICK OFF 80-81

DESIGN IT! 82-83

CLONE TYCOON 2 84-85

ASSASSIN! 86-87

SWORDBURST ONLINE 88-89

ACHIEVEMENT CHECKLIST 90-93

GOODBYE! 94-95

I INTRO

HALT! YOU THERE!

Yes, you look like precisely the type of person who could become a fine adventurer one day. But do not make haste just yet – one should never charge into battle without adequate preparation. You're liable to lose a limb if you're lucky, or your life if you're not.

However, it just so happens that my gallant knights have been putting together a collection of schemes, advice, and proposals to allow you to more easily survive the perils of Robloxia and conquer its many corners. In the subsequent pages I relay that wisdom to you. With the enclosed information at your disposal, you'll have no problem surviving post-apocalyptic landscapes, assuming the role of a hero in a supervillain-infested cityscape, or even cleaning the headquarters of a mysterious business ... my comrades have assured me that this last one will make sense once you've read this mighty tome.

And with that, brave trailblazer, I bid you success on a bountiful journey. Do be sure to heed the advice contained within, and venture forth with your own battalion of allies to aid you in your quest.

REDCLIFF ELITE COMMANDER

TREELANDS

Hidden deep underneath the canopy of a forgotten forest lies the peaceful world of TreeLands, where there's a treehouse with your name on it. TreeLands lets you harvest and trade a variety of fruit, zip around in an array of awesome vehicles, and create the ultimate treetop home.

TreeLands is home to a host of other treehouse-dwellers, as well as the residents of the main village. The central building is home to NewFissy and Suhreen, who will pay you for every fruit you bring to them.

There are tons of fruits to discover and trade back in the village, and they can be found all over the land. Some, like apples, are quite common, while others might require a long trek and a pinch of luck to find.

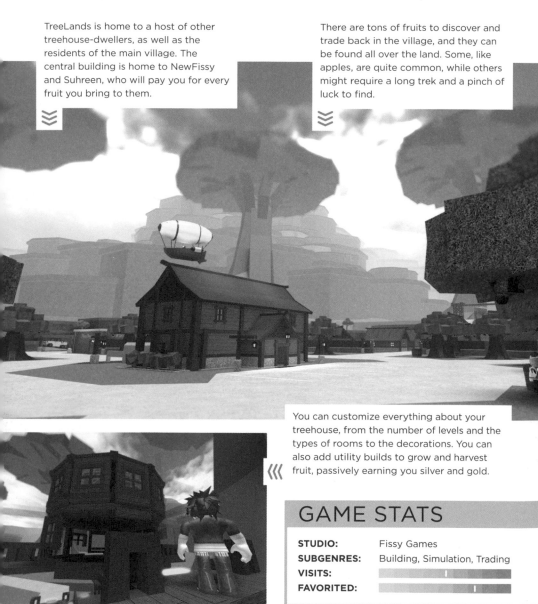

You can customize everything about your treehouse, from the number of levels and the types of rooms to the decorations. You can also add utility builds to grow and harvest fruit, passively earning you silver and gold.

GAME STATS

STUDIO:	Fissy Games
SUBGENRES:	Building, Simulation, Trading
VISITS:	
FAVORITED:	

QUICK TIPS

COMBINING
Make use of the combining baskets to create a gigantic super-fruit before you move on to the next tree. You can even uncombine the super-fruit and then recombine it to make bigger and more valuable fruits.

WAYPOINT
Harvesters earn you gold, but require you to pick certain fruit to unlock. In the harvest tab of the build menu, select a harvester, then press locate. An arrow will point you in the direction of the fruit!

BASE BEACON
It's important to make your treehouse stand out so you can easily find your way back home. Customize yours with distinctive features like lampposts, observation globes, and teleporters.

VEHICLES
You might find traveling a bit slow, but there are vehicles to help you get around. You can float around in a blimp or gyrocopter, or trundle along in a cargo truck that can transport your valuable wares.

NEWFISSY

One half of development group Fissy Games, and the creator of the TreeLands experience, NewFissy has been developing on Roblox since 2011. Below we discuss the importance and influence of the game's community, and how to make his already immensely popular game even better.

ON THE IMPORTANCE OF COMMUNITY
What's the most important game element to NewFissy? "No matter how technically brilliant or how dazzlingly beautiful, a game without a strong community of players will not succeed." There's a community of millions, in NewFissy's words, "one click away from connecting to, and playing, your game."

ON GIVING HIS COMMUNITY A SAY
Communities are important to TreeLands, and NewFissy often heeds their collective wisdom. "Every decision I've made for TreeLands after alpha testing was at least partially informed by the community. Every 5 minutes or so I'll get pinged with suggestions for TreeLands, and many of them actually make it into the game."

ON NEXT STEPS FOR TREELANDS
TreeLands was released in beta in early 2016, and players have been craving updates and consuming them as soon as they appear. So where will the roots of TreeLands spread next? "We have so many things planned for TreeLands: (1) Xbox support (2) Baskets that save fruit in your treehouse (3) A biplane." All of these features appear on the list of most-requested features by the community.

APOCALYPSE RISING

It's the end of the world as you know it in Apocalypse Rising, and a handful of survivors, yourself included, have taken refuge in the relative safety of Kin, a small town in the middle of nowhere. Do you have what it takes to endure the armageddon, or will another survivor get the better of you?

You spawn on a huge map, surrounded by rolling hills, with just a pistol and a flashlight to help you out. You might hear the odd groan of a zombie, or see the skies open with pouring rain, too.

Abandoned buildings are valuable places to scavenge. They often hold food, drink, and medicine to replenish health, weapons, and ammo to increase your firepower, or supplies for vehicles and structures.

Unusually speedy zombies lurk around every corner, but that's not all you have to watch out for. Every player is out to survive, so beware of other players – they may try to kill you and loot your items.

If you survive long enough to collect adequate supplies, you may be able to build a fortress from which to stave off zombies and players alike. You can also leave space for your vehicles, and store your surplus items.

GAME STATS

DEVELOPERS:	Gusmanak and ZolarKeth
SUBGENRES:	Survival, PvP, Shooter
VISITS:	
FAVORITED:	

QUICK TIPS

PACKING LIGHT
Managing your inventory is a difficult task when you have to balance so many different needs. Find a bag like the military backpack to give you more inventory slots and make scavenging easier.

CO-OP MODE
Enlist a trusted teammate to cover your back when you're out and about. Working in pairs or groups makes collecting items easy, as your buddies can take out any approaching zombies or players.

HANDY WEAPONS
Melee weapons like the crowbar are invaluable when you're in a bind. You don't need to replenish ammo, so they can get you out of tight spots and they're great for taking down the undead hordes.

HEADSHOT
Don't waste your precious ammo peppering zombies with bullets. A single well-placed shot to the head with most guns should be enough to put a zombie down for the count. Hopefully, at least.

GUSMANAK

The brain behind "Apoc" has welcomed over 100 million players to his zombie-infested dystopia. Not content with just one smash-hit game, Gusmanak is now hard at work on a sequel. We hear from the man himself on picking up development skills, sequel improvements, and becoming a team player.

ON WORKING AS A TEAM
An expansive game like Apocalypse Rising is the product of more than one person. Talking about his role in the team, Gusmanak says, "Most of my job is managing the team. For me, it's finding the right person and working with them the best I can. I'm getting better at running a tight ship."

ON CONTRIBUTING TO ROBLOX
Making games, building levels or designing items is hard work, but Gusmanak believes Roblox makes it simple. "It's easy to get started in any one area. If you want to practice scripting, you can test a studio place in minutes. If you want to make clothing, same thing. If you want to design a level, uploading and testing is a breeze."

ON ADVICE FOR SURVIVING APOC
"Don't trust anyone," is his suggestion for lasting a long time in the ruthless post-apocalyptic landscape. The PvP element of the game is one of its main attractions, but it's not without its flaws. "The game's group system allows the leader to kick a member instantly, so they're removed and killed without warning. Apoc 2 won't allow this."

JAILBREAK

Pick a life of crime or side with the law in Jailbreak, an open-world game of cat and mouse. As a police officer, your role is to maintain order in the prison and keep the inmates in line. Or you can don an orange jumpsuit and become a prisoner, hatching plans to escape to the city and a life of freedom.

⫷ As a prison officer, it's your job to keep prisoners on schedule and shepherd them around. If they step out of line, you can handcuff or stun them with your laser electrocutor.

⫷ If you've opted to play as a prisoner, bide your time and wait for an opportunity to escape. You don't start with any weapons, so you're outgunned ... but not necessarily outsmarted.

Helicopters are an officer's best friend – they can reach fugitives in a matter of seconds and allow access to rooftops. Don't worry if you fall, either – you've packed your automatic parachute!

There's a wide world for an escapee to explore. Grab some wheels and cruise around, rob a bank, or rent a safe house. Just be wary of patrolling officers, who want you back behind bars.

GAME STATS

STUDIO:	Badimo
SUBGENRES:	Town and City, Shooter, RPG
VISITS:	
FAVORITED:	

Written by Alex Wiltshire and Craig Jelley
Edited by Craig Jelley
Designed by John Stuckey and Andrea Philpots
Illustrations by Ryan Marsh, John Stuckey and Joe Bolder
Production by Louis Harvey
Special thanks to the entire Roblox team

All statistics featured in this title were based on information publicly available on the
Roblox platform and were correct as of March 2018.

ISBN 978-0-06-286266-2

19 20 21 22 RTLO 10 9 8 7 6 5 4 3 2
❖
First US Edition, 2018

Stay safe online. Any website addresses listed in this book are correct at the time of going to
print. However, HarperCollins is not responsible for content hosted by third parties. Please be
aware that online content can be subject to change and websites can contain content that is
unsuitable for children. We advise that all children are supervised when using the internet.

ROBLOX

QUICK TIPS

KEY SKILLS
As a prisoner, you need to get your hands on a keycard to open doors throughout the prison complex. Press the action button behind an unsuspecting officer to steal one.

BOUNTY HUNTER
If a police officer's salary isn't enough for you, then you can make a little extra money on the side by bringing in escaped criminals. The more notorious the criminal, the greater the reward.

INCOGNITO
Just committed the perfect bank job, but the police are on your tail? Take your car into a garage and get a new paint job to throw the cops off your scent. It should work for a little while at least ...

EJECTOR SEAT
Chasing criminals in cars can be tiresome, but police have the power to eject perps from their cars. Equip the handcuffs and press the action button to force the driver and passenger out.

BADIMO

Jailbreak collaborators asimo3089 and badcc, collectively known as Badimo, joined Roblox in the early days and grew up with it alongside many other creators, which helped foster a sense of community among themselves. Here they explain their experiences and give advice for new creators.

ON CREATING OVER PLAYING
"I never really played video games when I was younger," says badcc. "Sometimes I'd watch my friends play, but all I could think of was how I could make them, or make them better. I have more fun creating!"

ON NOSTALGIA
"It's so easy to get nostalgic about the old games from the 2009-2010 era," says asimo3089. "These games would not hold up today but there was something very special about them. They made great use of Roblox limitations and offered really exciting gameplay for their size." For badcc, it was less about the games than the makers of them. "I used to love meeting and talking to the creators of games about how they made certain things," he says.

ON THINKING TOO BIG
The pair have a warning for creators wanting to make games on the scale they do. "The most difficult thing to do is also really easy: going too big. I believe in pushing Roblox to its limits but pushing yourself too hard is a great way to get burned out," says asimo3089. "I'm always telling myself and badcc to keep it simple!" badcc agrees: "You'll never finish if you go overboard. Figure out what's worth your time. Time is the most valuable quantity in the world."

SHARK ATTACK!

What better respite from the adrenaline of adventuring than a short trip to a serene island? Oh wait, it's encircled by dozens of bloodthirsty sharks? Never mind then. Grab your trusty blade, enlist the help of a friendly pet, and dive foolishly into the waters of Shark Attack!

There are two stores on the main island – The Gem Shack, where you can trade in salvaged gems for coins, and The Shop, which sells all the survival essentials.

The waters are a deadly place, so everyone has their own boat to cruise around in, avoiding the perils that lurk beneath. There's a lot of ocean to explore and the boat is the quickest way to see it all.

There are different types of sharks to hunt, from the tiny bull shark to the megalodon – a prehistoric monstrosity that dwarfs all others. Every shark has its own strength and health stats, making each a different challenge.

If you're sufficiently daring you can dive into the water and hunt for gems and treasure. Just make sure to keep an eye on the bubble, which represents your oxygen level. If it disappears, then you'll drown!

GAME STATS

DEVELOPER:	FuzzyWooo
SUBGENRES:	Fighting, Monster, Trading
VISITS:	
FAVORITED:	

QUICK TIPS

HIDDEN GEMS
Find gems in the water by looking out for colorful glows. Dive down when you see one, and the gem will be sparkling beneath. Grab it quickly before the sharks smell blood!

GONE FISHING
Cast your rod to snare fish, then roast them on a campfire to make them edible. The next time you get bitten by a shark, you'll have tons of fish with which to recover your health.

FAST FOOD
Sharks are faster than you, so if you're stranded in the water with one, hold the jump button to reach safety. You may get nipped a few times, but you'll make it harder for a shark to bite you.

PET PALS
Although unable to cause much damage, a pet can mean the difference between life and death. Buy one as soon as you can, whether it's a tiny turtle, or your very own great white!

FUZZYWOOO

FuzzyWooo was introduced to Roblox by her kids in 2015. After experimenting with clothing design, she began to explore making games and was surprised how straightforward it was. Here she explains why managing time is important, and the pleasures of looking back on how far her game has come.

ON KEEPING IT IN THE FAMILY
FuzzyWooo's love for art ultimately led her toward the game creation potential of Roblox, where she began by creating maps. "Eventually my son, GrandSnaf, joined me in making my games come to life by scripting my ideas for me. Together we created Shark Attack!, which is my most popular game."

ON UTILIZING TIME
"For me, the most difficult thing about game development is time management," FuzzyWooo says. When she starts on a new project, she doesn't like to stop until she's finished. "This sometimes doesn't bode well when the project has an expected completion time frame of two weeks. I have to find sleep at some point, even though my desire to create is running full-speed ahead of me."

ON ONGOING DEVELOPMENT
Rather than pinpoint one particular feature of Shark Attack! as being her favorite, FuzzyWooo is proud of how it's evolved since release. "I look back at its beginnings and shudder that people actually enjoyed it!" she says. "It has come a long way from its very humble beginnings of a very basic map and sharks with a lipstick-like mouth to a more detailed map with animated sharks that actually open their mouths to bite!"

NATURAL DISASTER SURVIVAL

Prepare for the worst and hope for the best. Natural Disaster Survival leaves you with just your own ingenuity and tasks you with braving a variety of elements on multiple maps. It's a game of tactics, luck, and running around wildly in circles, screaming your head off.

Each round is set on a unique map, from the Surf Central beach to the Rakish Refinery industrial hub. It'll take a few rounds to work out the perfect survival spots on each map.

Other players can both help and hinder you. If you're on a new map, players will often flock to the safest spots. However, they can also block the best spots, or nudge you from a precarious perch.

Disasters generate at random each round, and range from a blizzard's icy gusts to plummeting meteors. Each has a different survival condition, whether it's seeking high ground or dodging falling objects.

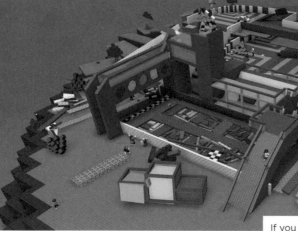

If you perish during a round, you'll reenter the hub to await the next map. From here you can see the action unfold on the island, check out the leaderboard, and hatch a plan to leapfrog whoever's above you.

GAME STATS

DEVELOPER:	Stickmasterluke
SUBGENRES:	Party, Survival
VISITS:	
FAVORITED:	

QUICK TIPS

HORSEPOWER
Some maps contain vehicles such as tractors, go-karts, and trucks. In addition to being fun to ride, they may also help you avoid some disasters due to their increased speed, such as when you're trying to avoid meteors.

PARAMOUNT
At the start of a round, try to get to higher ground as quickly as possible. An elevated spot may be unnecessary, but it is good in many disasters and it's easier to reach when there's no one else up there fighting for a spot.

MULTI MAYHEM
Sometimes you may encounter a map that has more than one disaster. In these instances, try to find a spot that will avoid the most disasters – avoid acid rain indoors in a skyscraper that will also survive a flood, for example.

DISASTER MASTER
After a few rounds you might find simply surviving becomes a little too easy. Set yourself an additional challenge for each type of disaster. For example, how close can you get to the top of a volcano without perishing?

STICKMASTERLUKE

Stickmasterluke started building things in Roblox during the early days of the platform, using it as a way of showing his creations off to his friends. Here he explains the joys of destruction, the lure of distractions, and how you can use any idea as inspiration for a game.

ON GETTING DISTRACTED
What's the trickiest thing about making games? "For me, staying on task," says Stickmasterluke. "The quality of games on Roblox is getting higher, to a point where the little details matter." He's increasingly getting sidetracked by new ideas while he's polishing his current game!

ON UNEXPECTED INSPIRATION
Many devs suggest that new creators start with a game mechanic, but Stickmasterluke believes there shouldn't be limits. "Games is the medium with the highest variety, so game development

can start anywhere," he says. "It can start with a story that you want to tell,' a genre that you are interested in, or a mechanic that you want to explore. And with every start you can branch it, fill it in, and mix it in any way you like."

ON BREAKING THINGS
He's most proud of NDS's destructibility: "I think everyone can find joy in watching the ways structures can be destroyed. As a map is torn apart, you can see all the pieces that made it up, how they interact with each other, and how they made something better than its individual parts."

INNOVATION LABS

Deep below ground, there lies a clandestine facility dedicated to scientific advancement. However, it's often mere minutes away from meltdown. It's your duty as part of the Innovation Labs team to contain the experiments, prevent the core from exploding, and ultimately save the day.

Innovation Labs is made up of sectors, from the seemingly safe Food Lab to the sinister Genetic Reconstruction department. Just what is the lab's aim? It's up to you to piece together the mystery!

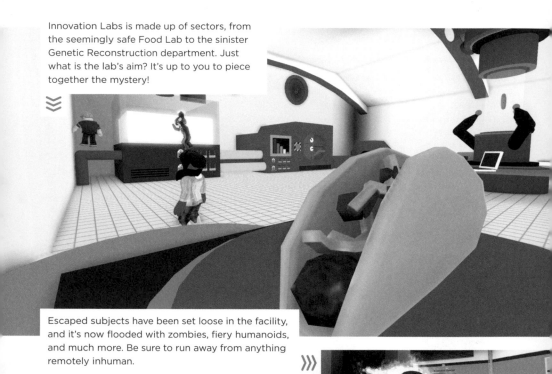

Escaped subjects have been set loose in the facility, and it's now flooded with zombies, fiery humanoids, and much more. Be sure to run away from anything remotely inhuman.

Your aim is to keep the facility core secure from the dangers within, as well as from clumsy fellow players. If it blows, the game is over – until the nanobots repair the labs for the umpteenth time!

GAME STATS

DEVELOPER:	madattak
SUBGENRES:	Sci-Fi, Mystery, Exploration
VISITS:	
FAVORITED:	

QUICK TIPS

LABYRINTH

Keep an eye out for ladders and crawlspaces in the labs. These can be used to access secret areas, provide shortcuts between sectors, or as hiding spaces from whatever menace happens to be stalking you.

SUBTLE NODS

There are dozens of easter eggs hidden around the gigantic facility, referencing famous games and films, among other things. One of them even alludes to an alleged chicken thief, who has been hiding amongst the Roblox team.

DE-ZOMBIFICATION

If you're infected by a zombified monster, you'll begin to slump and shamble through the facility. To cure yourself of this ailment, find the disinfection chamber and let its cleansing gamma rays wash over you.

SHINE A LIGHT

Some of the laboratory can be quite dark and hard to make out, particularly when the core is beginning to shut down. Get your hands on a flashlight to help you make sense of this chaotic establishment.

MADATTAK

Innovation Labs rocketed madattak into the development stratosphere and quickly became his most popular game, surpassing previous efforts, Innovation HQ and Build a Plane Challenge. He reveals his tricks to surviving development, becoming a better developer, and leaving ideas behind.

ON COMPLETING GAMES

Enthusiasm can dwindle when working on a long project, but madattak prescribes one thing to keep going: "Confidence. You make good progress on a project, and then you start to doubt yourself, or feel like it's a bad idea that will never succeed. Overcoming this feeling is one of the hardest parts of completing any game."

ON PUSHING HIS LIMITS

"The core meltdown was a huge step up from the coding I was doing previously," he says of Innovation Labs' impressive endgame. Most players who have experienced this stage of the game would agree that the panic and chaos of the meltdown "created a dramatic experience that was quite unique for Roblox at the time."

ON CUTTING HIS LOSSES

Not every idea works out quite so successfully, however, and some ideas had to be cut. "There was an entire rocket silo and control room that allowed you to fire a huge rocket," he says. "In the end the whole area was cut, as launching the rocket was always underwhelming; it never felt powerful or dramatic."

ROBLOX DEATHRUN

Take part in a footrace to the death in Roblox Deathrun! As you and your fellow racers charge through a variety of maps, one rotten spoilsport is operating a sinister system of traps to send you to your doom. Reach the end, however, and you can exact revenge for your fallen allies.

At the start of the game you'll be dropped into the lobby, which is basically a big playground in itself. Here you can run and jump around the various areas, check the leaderboards, or buy weapons and trails at one of the shops.

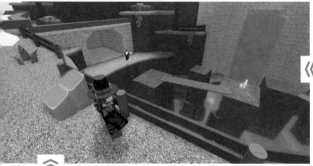

Each map is situated in its own world and has different traps to overcome. The killer occupies the central area to easily control the surrounding traps, while the runners follow the course to an endpoint, which will transport them to the killer's area.

During each run, you can earn experience and points for every coin you collect, checkpoint you reach, player you kill (if you're controlling the traps), and for finally ending the killer's reign of terror and winning the round.

GAME STATS

STUDIO:	Team Deathrun
SUBGENRES:	PvP, Obby, Racing
VISITS:	
FAVORITED:	

QUICK TIPS

SLOW AND STEADY
Being at the front of the pack will mean you're likely to be hit with all the traps. Hang back a little, let someone set traps off first, then zoom past. Repeat this through the course and you should at least be able to finish!

CLOSE-UP
Other runners can sometimes get in your way and block your view of the way ahead, which is less than ideal on an intricate obby course. Zoom your camera in as close as possible to avoid too many of these obstructions.

NO MERCY
When you get the chance to play as the killer, make sure you watch the runners carefully as they approach each obstacle. You only get one shot at most traps, so time that button-press perfectly for maximum effect.

KILLERWATCH
After playing a couple of games as the killer, you'll begin to get an idea of where the traps are and what they do. When you play as a runner again, watch the killer to see if they're close to setting off a nearby trap.

WSLY

As the leader of Team Deathrun, Wsly has been the driving force behind the trap-riddled obby smash-hit since 2010, winning an armful of awards in the process. What inspired him to begin creating? To whom does he partially owe Deathrun's success? What secrets does he hold about Deathrun? Find out below.

ON BEGINNING DEVELOPMENT
What put Wsly on the path to becoming a superstar developer? "Roblox did!" However, he was inspired long before he discovered the platform. "I played games such as SimCity and Rollercoaster Tycoon and built large moveable contraptions with LEGO and K'NEX toys."

ON TEAM EFFORT
Deathrun's maps are among the most unique and inventive to be found on Roblox, and Wsly puts that down to the unique strengths of a multitude of different contributors. "There are a

lot of maps, animations, assets, and scripts in the game made by over 10 developers. This makes the game a large collaborative art project in which we all have our own share."

ON HIDDEN HELP
Not everything in Deathrun is as apparent as the deadly traps; in fact, there are some helpful objects on the courses, too. As Wsly points out, "There are various interactive objects scattered throughout the levels that you can pick up by walking against them. These objects can be very helpful to get around traps." Very handy indeed.

M☾☾N TYC☾☾N

Build a moon base, engineer a thriving economy, and capture planets under your flag. In this galactic tycoon game, other players are a threat to your plans for dominion, so you must balance resources between developing your base and buying powerful guns to fight them off.

Start by building a conveyor, then mine minerals by clicking the green button. Click until you've earned enough for your first automatic moon drop.

Continue investing in moon and beam drops to keep the money flowing. When you can afford it, build a ship to fly to the planets above your base.

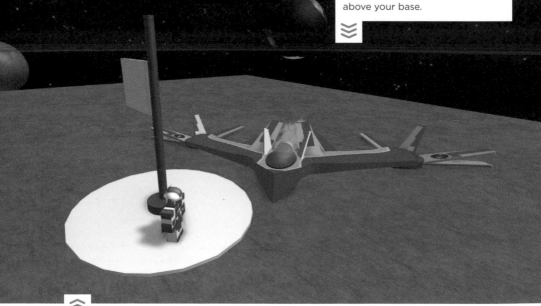

On each planet is a flag, which you can capture. Simply stand next to it to make it yours, and make sure the enemy doesn't take it back!

GAME STATS

DEVELOPER:	Lethal682
SUBGENRES:	Sci-Fi, Tycoon, Fighting
VISITS:	
FAVORITED:	

QUICK TIPS

DEFEND YOURSELF
Look out for other players! Buy walls for your base as soon as you can to ensure you're safe as you work, and invest in the best guns you can buy to deter or damage invaders.

BANK JOB
The Enhancer will give a huge boost to your mineral income, so purchase one as early as you can. This will mean a constant steady income that can be used to build up your base.

DEFENDER
Your ship has guns and missiles, but be aware that it's very vulnerable to gunfire from other players. Take care when you attempt to land on an occupied planet so you can avoid being hit.

SPAWN SAFE
If you're repeatedly being killed on your base before you've built walls, remember that you're invincible when you respawn. Stay still, wait, and soon enough they'll leave you alone.

LETHAL682

Moon Tycoon was Lethal682's first front page game. Before Roblox came along, he had no idea that he could actually make his ideas into games for himself and have millions of people play them! Here he explains how he gets started, and discusses a surprising source of material in Moon Tycoon …

ON PLANNING A NEW GAME

"Know what your genre is and who your audience is," Lethal682 wisely advises. "Think about the mechanics of the game and how they will work. I like to jot my ideas out under different headings such as: mechanics, features, challenges, and replayability."

ON THINKING SMALL

Once you have an idea, Lethal682 says that starting small is a good idea. "Don't try to develop the entire game all at once. Start by solving smaller problems to see how your game works, and keep working on that design to build the foundation of your game." With a solid core

system it's easier, he says, to stay motivated as you continue to add more to it. "You'll find that your game will start to piece together without you even realizing it. After starting, everything begins to flow and game development becomes really enjoyable. It's an overwhelming feeling to see your ideas come to life, and this motivates you even more. So get started!"

ON MAKING SOUND EFFECTS

Sometimes you have to get creative when you're making a game, as Lethal682 illustrates: "In Moon Tycoon I couldn't find any good sound effects for a weapon, so I used the sound of a typewriter to mimic it!"

IMPERIUM

Travel back in time to the medieval kingdom of Imperium and forge your own legend, collecting resources, gold, and comrades along the way. Wander between towns and trade as a merchant, quell fearsome threats as a warrior, or command a legion as a supreme royal leader.

You're dropped into the town of Cambria with nothing but a few tools to aid you. Your first job is to collect some resources. Chop trees with an axe, cut down crops with a sickle, or mine with a pickaxe to receive wood, food, or stone.

The inhabitants of the kingdom can help you out on your journey. The stockhouse master will trade your resources for gold, the blacksmith can forge better tools and deadly weapons, and the stablemaster will rent out space for your steed.

Once you have enough resources and gold, you can purchase a plot of land in any of the three main towns and build a home for yourself. To begin with, you'll only have access to a simple house, but you can upgrade to a whole castle when you have more resources.

GAME STATS

STUDIO:	Imperator
SUBGENRES:	Medieval, Fighting, Crafting
VISITS:	
FAVORITED:	

QUICK TIPS

LOST IN TIME

The kingdom is a humongous place and easy to get lost in when you're felling a forest or disappearing down a mine. Consult the world map to identify waypoints that you can use to navigate your way back to town.

TRADE TRAVELS

If you're in no hurry to get rid of hard-earned resources, check out how much you can sell each of them for in the three different towns. Some of the stockhouse masters will pay more gold for certain resources than others.

BOUNTY HUNTER

Being hunted by a stronger enemy but don't have any allies to call upon? You can create bounties on the town notice boards for a minimum of 1000 gold. If you're feeling helpful, you can also take them on for the same fee!

WEAPON MASTER

The blacksmith has dozens of different weapons to suit your play style. Will you get up close and personal with a short sword, charge on horseback with a halberd, or pick people off from a distance with a ranged bow?

ROYTT

Roytt started playing Roblox and using Studio back in 2009, but only started making full games recently. Not that this has slowed him down for a moment! Read on as he explains why he wishes he started creating games earlier, and where he finds his best inspiration.

ON MAKING RATHER THAN PLAYING

"I've always been the creative type," Roytt says. "I always enjoyed making stuff rather than playing games." When he started on Roblox, he spent time drawing and creating structures. "I guess the ease of learning and the lively community got me into developing for Roblox."

ON REGRETS

"I wish I had gotten into game development earlier," he continues. Roytt only started scripting a few years ago and admits he still has a lot to learn. "I really enjoy it now and I often

think how much more I would have liked it if I had picked it up a bit earlier!"

ON INSPIRATION

Roytt finds the best source of ideas outside Roblox, and even outside games in general. "Most of the time I find myself listening to music or reading a book and I'm inspired by the melody or some powerful sentence someone has written," he says. "From there an idea comes that will work as the base for a project and will be refined during development by different sources of inspiration."

MOUNT OF THE GODS

Balance your own needs with those of the almighty beings who preside over your tiny island in Mount of the Gods. Turn your remote paradise into a bustling colony by recruiting friends to harvest crops, raise cattle, and build structures – just make sure not to anger the omnipotent ones …

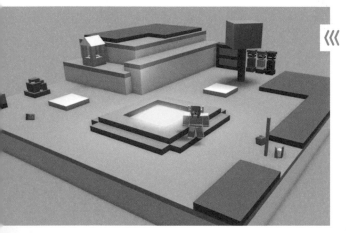

You'll begin on a deserted island, with few available resources and a boiling hot lava pit beside you. The pit is where sacrifices are offered to the gods – crops and resources are accepted!

When seasons pass, and if the gods are happy, the land will grow outward and you will be granted more resources, from cows and corn seeds, to ore veins and apple trees.

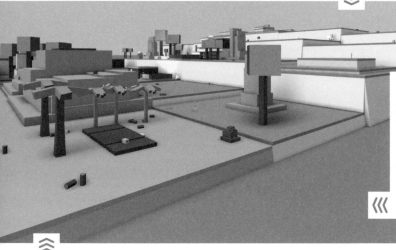

To build, approach a plot and press the action button. This will bring up a list of possible constructions and the items you need to build them. The crafting table is particularly useful initially to create tools.

As your island swells, it's harder to collect the scattered resources you need before the season's end. Enlist friends to help out, and determine a role for each – farmer, cattle wrangler, crafter, and so on.

GAME STATS

DEVELOPER:	Wheatlies
SUBGENRES:	Fighting, Crafting, Tycoon
VISITS:	
FAVORITED:	

QUICK TIPS

BEHIND THE MASK

When you enter a game, you'll be able to select a mask, some of which can imbue bonuses on the player, although many of them have to be unlocked. Check the description of each mask to find out how to unlock them.

WINTER IS COMING

Though all the seasons offer some resources, winter is the most barren in terms of crops. Make sure you prepare for the lull in the seasons by keeping a store to one side, so you still have enough to offer to the gods.

WELLING UP

Your starter island has a conveniently situated well to quench thirst, but as the island expands, it's harder to locate. Make sure to build extra wells all over your island so you and your fellow castaways can always have a drink.

SNEAK ATTACK

As the island grows, there are more spaces for dangerous creatures to lurk. Prepare yourself by forging a sword on a crafting table and storing it on your back in case of an ambush by scorpions, spiders, or a pride of lions!

WHEATLIES

Wheatlies doesn't only have experience making games on Roblox. Having dabbled with other game development platforms, Roblox is the one to which he keeps returning. Here he explains how he started out designing games on paper, and why he was right to listen to his 14-year-old self!

ON MAKING GAMES ON PAPER

Wheatlies made games before he could code. "I would sit down and write a bunch of rules and get my cousins to test them, kind of like creating primitive board games," he says. On discovering Roblox, he realized, "I could use code to create practically anything I wanted!"

ON WHY ROBLOX IS SPECIAL

"Roblox has a special place in my heart as a developer," says Wheatlies. "It has become an ecosystem that I understand on a different level." He appreciates the powerful tools Roblox provides, which other engines expect developers to make themselves. "It's the best place to publish anything, in my opinion. You can have hundreds of people playing your thing in a few minutes, which is a really special experience."

ON HEEDING HIS 14-YEAR-OLD SELF

MotG is based on a game Wheatlies made when he was 14. "The original is very wonky, but I loved the idea so much and I kept coming back to it," he says. "It wasn't until I was 19 that I actually managed to do it again. Sometimes these things stay with you for a reason."

NEVERLAND LAGOON

Visit the haven of Neverland Lagoon, where fairies, mermaids, and pirates coexist peacefully ... most of the time. This magical world lets you and your friends create a new character and your own adventures, as you swim, fly, and hunt for Buck-Eye the Pirate's legendary treasure.

You'll spawn in a castle, where you can customize your character with morphs, which allow you to dress up in mermaid tails, fairy wings, and dozens of outfits. You can adapt the colors of each part using the charts on the wall, too.

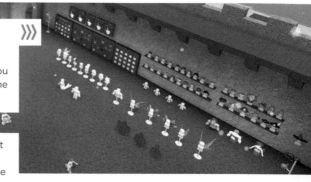

The land of Neverland Lagoon has distinct areas to explore and role-play in. You can hop aboard a bustling galleon at the Pirate Coast, visit the quaint village of FeyDorf, or grab a drink at the local tavern.

There are dozens of hidden areas to explore and secrets to discover. Descend into the underwater caves to see what you can find, or talk to Buck-Eye the Pirate to begin a quest laden with treasure.

GAME STATS

DEVELOPERS:	SelDraken & Teiyia
SUBGENRES:	RPG, Fantasy
VISITS:	
FAVORITED:	

QUICK TIPS

CHATTERBOX
Talk to everyone you meet, as they always have something interesting to say. Some of them might give you inspiration for an adventure, while others may disclose hints that will lead you to one of Neverland Lagoon's secrets.

INTERACTION
The amazing scenery isn't just there to make the lagoon look pretty – you can interact with a lot of what you see. Try hopping on the swings by the lagoon, or shooting a cannon at the Pirate Coast.

LAZY BABY
One of the morphs turns you into a baby character, which allows other normal-sized players to pick you up and carry you around. It's perfect if you want to explore the expansive world but don't want to press any buttons ...

GRIN AND BEAR IT
Don't stray too far into the outskirts of the world. Fearsome bears patrol the perimeter and will attack on sight. Your sword and blunderbuss aren't at all effective against them so the best option is to run away very quickly!

SELDRAKEN

Many of Roblox's makers are new to making games, but SelDraken has been making them for decades! Here he explains how Roblox compares to the early days of gaming, and why he's proud of a feature he worked hard to create, which Roblox has since made much easier to accomplish!

ON GAME MAKING, 1985-STYLE
SelDraken got his first computer, an Apple IIc, in 1985, at 12. "Looking at a blank screen, with one little blinking cursor in the bottom left corner, just waiting for me to give it a command ... it was as if a whole world had opened to me," he says. His dad bought him magazines that listed code that he would copy line-by-line.

ON TIMELESS EXCITEMENT
"Even now, when I get into an empty project on Roblox, with that gray baseplate floating before me, that feeling of excitement at being able to let my imagination flow and create a world all of my own is the same as with my old Apple."

ON CREATIVE SOLUTIONS
It took two weeks to work out how to shrink characters down to the size of a baby, before R15 bodies revolutionized the way avatars worked! "At the time, for noobs as we were, that was a great accomplishment!" he says. "In hindsight, there may have been easier ways to do this than the bulk of code that I came up with for Neverland, but even today, it's this mechanism in the game that I am most proud of."

TRADELANDS

Don your tricorn, grab a musket, and set sail on the winds of Tradelands. Collect materials to build a seaworthy ship and ferry goods between islands for the East Robloxia Company, pocketing as many doubloons as you can. Like all good adventures, this is best with a crew of shipmates.

(((Your adventure begins aground, and you have just a few tools with which to build your ocean-faring empire. Mine iron using a pickaxe, use the axe to chop down trees, and you'll soon have stacks of resources.

Talk to the dockmaster to spawn your ship, then set sail. You can navigate to new islands using the map, but beware of ships from other factions. They may try to sink your ship (((and plunder your loot!

Store your resources at the town warehouse, then visit a shipwright. If you have enough iron and oak, you'll be able to build your first ship. As you gain more resources and doubloons (((you'll gain access to much better ships.

Earn doubloons by shipping goods between ports for the East Robloxia Company. If you're a crew member rather than the (((captain, you'll still receive a cut of the haul.

GAME STATS

DEVELOPER:	Nahr_Nahrstein
SUBGENRES:	Naval, Exploration, Trading
VISITS:	
FAVORITED:	

QUICK TIPS

OVERBOARD
When you're sailing, make sure not to jump as you could fall off your ship. If there are no crew members to stop it, the ship will carry on sailing, leaving you to flounder in the water. Your ship could become a target for rival ships.

IRONCLAD
You can unlock access to better ships as you level up. These vessels have more space for cargo and cannons, as well as better speed and durability. Some ships are even coated in armor to make them almost impenetrable.

UNLIMITED SUPPLIES
As you mine ores and fell trees, the durability of your tools decreases and they will eventually break. The town's general trader will give you new ones for free, so you can continue to collect valuable resources.

MOTLEY CREW
The pirate's life is best enjoyed with a crew behind you. Employ friends to man the cannons, navigate courses to new islands, or just do the heavy lifting of precious loot. They'll be paid handsomely for their efforts, of course.

NAHR_NAHRSTEIN

Beginning with the intention of making a flight simulator, Nahr_Nahrstein instead ended up with a game that went by sea rather than by sky, inspired by classic seafaring adventures. Here he explains how players shape Tradelands, and what he'd like to make next.

ON EXPLORING NEW GENRES
"I've always wanted to make a city role-play game like Welcome to Bloxburg or Urbis," he tells us. "I've had a lot of ideas on how to expand gameplay and make these games much more interesting." Sounds promising, but he's been too busy with other projects to get started.

ON PLAYERS STEERING THE GAME
Nahr_Nahrstein finds one of the big motivations to continue development on Tradelands has been the way the community plays the game. "Players are given the choice to play as one of four nations, and many players choose to stick with the same one for a long period of time, becoming involved with that faction's navy and politics," he says. "The rivalries between nations drive Tradelands' storyline and development."

ON LOCATING RARE MATERIALS
"Electrosteel can only be mined in storms on non-spawn islands, using an angelic sapphire pickaxe," he explains. "Angelwood can be collected from trees on non-spawn islands using a golden axe, and sapphires can be collected on the same islands using a golden pickaxe."

PRISON LIFE

You're back behind bars – but for how long this time? Choose between the guard and prisoner factions and try to quell or create chaos in the prison. Which side ultimately prevails is up to you. Coordinate your team, take your opportunities, and you may just get to leave the prison alive.

(((As a prisoner, your goal is to find a way out of the facility. The only way out is to get your hands on a guard's keycard. Bide your time, keep to your schedule, and look for items that can give you a chance to escape.

(((Guards can choose from an inventory that includes laser electrocutors, cuffs, and shotguns. They also have an access-all-areas keycard and a surveillance room.

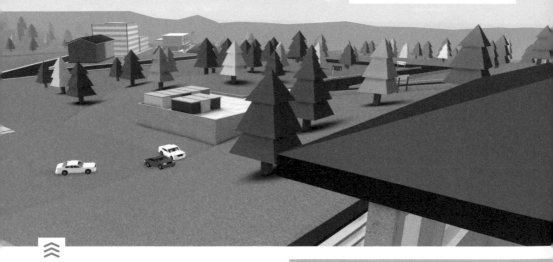

The lawless land beyond the prison is ruled by criminals – former prisoners who have thus far evaded the long arm of the law. They can cause havoc for prisoners and guards alike, as they tend to get rowdy and infiltrate the prison.

GAME STATS

DEVELOPER:	Aesthetical
SUBGENRES:	Town and City, Shooter, Survival
VISITS:	
FAVORITED:	

QUICK TIPS

BIG BROTHER
The surveillance room has multiple cameras that can be used to keep an eye on different areas of the prison. Use these views in coordination with the chat windows to effectively mobilize your team from a central location.

KEY TO FAILURE
If you're playing as a guard, make sure to check that the coast is clear before going through one of the secure doors. You may inadvertently provide prisoners with a route to freedom, or worse – direct access to the deadly armory.

INFINITE AMMO
All the weapons in Prison Life have unlimited ammo, so if you can't shoot, it just means you need to reload. Make sure that you get in the habit of doing this often, and especially before you enter a shoot-out or a criminal territory!

FREEDOM REIGNS
If you escape prison, you're now a criminal. Find a garage, where you can resupply weapons and spawn cars, then stand on the red platforms inside. If you die after this, you'll respawn at the garage, not prison!

AESTHETICAL

It took Aesthetical months to learn scripting in Roblox, but his games are a shining example of where practice can take you! Here he explains how his imagination guided him to Roblox, and how sometimes you have to accept what's good enough rather than your highest ambitions.

ON "GOOD ENOUGH"
You can't always make exactly what you want, as Aesthetical explains. "I take a lot of time in building and scripting, but often I find myself unsatisfied, so I delete everything and start over again. Iterating designs and code can be good but sometimes I can get a bit obsessed. Settling on a compromise between the ideal build and what's 'good enough' can be hard."

ON DAYDREAMING
"Since I was a kid, I've always daydreamed about random situations and scenarios, such as being a survivor of a plane crash or rappelling down a building as a secret agent. Doodles of the adventures I imagined covered every empty space in my school notes!" It wasn't until he discovered Roblox that he was able to turn these ideas into games.

ON ROBLOX'S SPECIAL SAUCE
"Roblox has a shallow learning curve compared to other game engines," he says. "It also takes care of the hard parts of game development, like multiplayer, so that you can focus on what matters most: making a game that you love."

TEMPLE OF MEMORIES

Explore a serene land full of cloud-encircled mountains, cherry blossom trees, and ancient Asian architecture in Temple of Memories. There's no aim other than to discover the secrets that are hidden throughout the land, so take your time, enjoy the scenery, and become a master of zen.

The world is inspired by the spiritual Far East. You'll see amazing temples, ponds filled with majestic koi, and pagodas upon mountaintops.

Meditation is how you earn zen, the world's currency. Press the animate button and stand still to earn zen, and reach a higher state of enlightenment.

Some areas are forbidden, even to those who have reached a state of nirvana. Look out for skull banners and don't cross them, or you'll be tossed aside by a mysterious force. It's easier to throw enlightened beings, you see ...

GAME STATS

DEVELOPER:	Crykee
SUBGENRES:	Exploration, Showcase
VISITS:	
FAVORITED:	

QUICK TIPS

ZEN MASTER

As you meditate and earn more zen, you'll unlock access to different meditation animations. You can select each one from the inventory screen and press animate to sample them individually before choosing your favorite.

SPIRITED AWAY

There are dozens of chests hidden all over the land, even underwater, so explore every nook and cranny to find them. Each chest you open will bestow upon you a colored spirit orb that will follow you everywhere you go.

CHEAT MODE

If all you have to do to earn zen is stay still, you can keep the game running while you do other things. When you return, you'll have more zen than you'll know what to do with. The spirits will know you're a zen fraud, though ...

ENLIGHTENED ONE

If a life of solemn meditation is truly how you wish to spend the rest of your life, then it's imperative that you look the part. You can purchase the relevant outfits, auras, and even the ability to fly from the in-game store.

CRYKEE

After spending hundreds of hours playing games on Roblox, Crykee soon got serious about the platform once he set his sights on joining Elite Builders of Robloxia, and he quickly improved his game! Here Crykee explains the joy of making friends and doing the minimum before going maximum.

ON MAKING NEW FRIENDS

"I love making connections with other people on Roblox," Crykee says. "Making friends when you don't expect it is great, from competing with each other, role-playing, or even just relaxing and having interesting conversations. The unpredictability of what'll happen after you join a game is what keeps me coming back."

ON MINIMAL VIABLE PRODUCTS

Crykee advises the first thing a creator should think about is a solid design. "This can be achieved by thinking about what you want out

of the game. Why are you creating it in the first place?" he says. After that, it's easy to add features. "You can start off by creating a minimal viable product to test the game with friends. If it isn't fun then take a step back and improve it."

ON CREATIVE FREEDOM

"Setting aside the amount of time it would take, I wish I had made Theme Park Tycoon," Crykee says. "I love the creative freedom it offers its players, similar to the experience of making things in Roblox itself. The community gets to choose how they want to experience the game."

HEROES OF ROBLOXIA

Robloxia is under attack from supervillains and only you and your team can save it. Jump into the pages of your own comic book–inspired adventure in Heroes of Robloxia, an episodic adventure game that pits you and your super-friends against Robloxia's greatest evils.

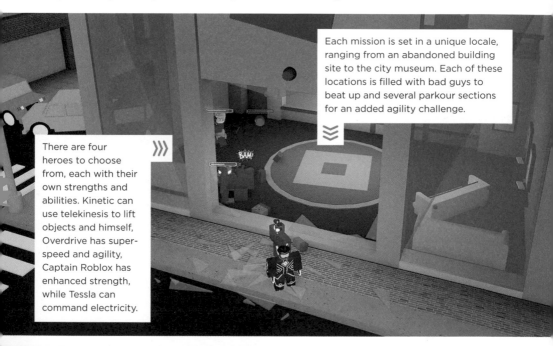

Each mission is set in a unique locale, ranging from an abandoned building site to the city museum. Each of these locations is filled with bad guys to beat up and several parkour sections for an added agility challenge.

There are four heroes to choose from, each with their own strengths and abilities. Kinetic can use telekinesis to lift objects and himself, Overdrive has super-speed and agility, Captain Roblox has enhanced strength, while Tessla can command electricity.

There's a supervillain pulling the strings and deploying his henchman on every mission. Experiment with different superteam combos to outwit each villain and imprison them back at HQ.

GAME STATS

STUDIO:	Team Super
SUBGENRES:	Fighting, Platformer
VISITS:	
FAVORITED:	

QUICK TIPS

HERO PARTY
Enlist your friends to aid your mission to take on the scourge of Robloxia, and you can make life a lot easier. There'll be more people to take down the henchmen at each location, and no need to switch characters for various scenarios.

ONE FOR ALL
If you're playing solo, you can switch between characters to adapt to situations, but note that they share a health bar. If you're in trouble, switch to Overdrive to make a quick getaway, or Tessla to attack from range.

MOBBED
Your health goes down faster when attacked by a whole group of enemies, so try and take them out one by one. You can do this by luring individual enemies away from a group, or by hitting them from a distance with ranged attacks.

SURPRISE ENDING
Defeat the final boss to reveal the conclusion to the comic-inspired story. Maybe the big bad wasn't so bad after all? Check back into HQ once you've beaten the final mission to see if there are any secrets to discover.

MASTEROFTHEELEMENTS

Lead developer of Team Super, MasterOfTheElements, started out on Roblox making clothes before he saw the potential in game creation and began working toward "something that had never been seen on Roblox before." Here he explains the true challenge that comes with realizing such ambitions.

ON MAINTAINING MOTIVATION
Having skills is great, but MasterOfTheElements reminds us that's not all you need. "You have to put in the endless hours to make it work, too, and after working on the same thing for what feels like years, the motivation that drove you in the beginning will fade. That's when you need the willpower to plow through, even if your motivation dips. Nobody thinks the same thing for a year straight. You will get different ideas, ideas that will feel a lot better than what you're currently working on. And that's when you face the dilemma: do you want to continue working on what you used to feel was a great game, or do you want to put it on pause and start something that is even greater?"

ON IDEAS
"No matter if you're a game developer or want to be one, everyone has ideas about 'the most amazing game that Roblox has ever seen,'" says MasterOfTheElements. "It doesn't matter if you've made five front page games, or your greatest achievement is reaching 1000 visits, everyone has great ideas. The problem comes when trying to realize them."

WOLVES' LIFE 2

Run wild in a lupine life simulator in which you can found or join a pack, explore a world full of mountains, lakes, and deserts, and claim a den. Play out your wolf life, socializing with the other inhabitants of the world, using the many ways to express your wolf self!

Familiarize yourself with the emotes available to play as a wolf, including everyday ones like eating, drinking, and sitting – and the silly ones, too!

There are many wolves to choose to play as. To begin, you can choose between three standard wolf varieties – normal, fluffy, and shorthair.

Scattered across the world are many dens. Lots of them will be occupied by other packs, but you should find an empty one you can claim as your own.

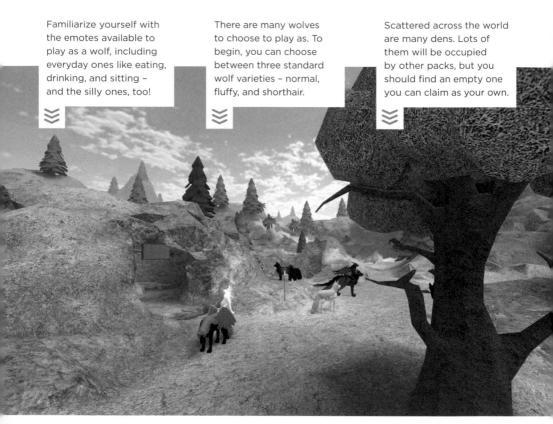

Every 12 hours you can attempt a Time Attack mode. You have six minutes to collect 100 gems scattered across the landscape.

GAME STATS

STUDIO:	Shyfoox studios
SUBGENRES:	RPG, Simulation
VISITS:	
FAVORITED:	

QUICK TIPS

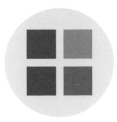

COAT OF PAINT
You have lots of power to customize your wolf at the start of the game. Choose its fur colors and even the color of its nose and ears. Use the advanced menu to decorate each part of your wolf in a different color.

AGE RATING
When creating your character, you can choose to play as adult or teen wolves, or even a pup. There's no difference between them in terms of abilities – instead they let you role-play as a family unit with your friends.

IN BLOOM
Find the flowers hidden around the map and walk into them to take their magical effects, such as sparkles of various colors, and elemental effects such as fire and ice. They'll certainly make you stand out from the pack!

SUPER WOOF
The Divine Wolf is very expensive, but comes with many powers. It emanates an ethereal glow and allows you to give commands to create fire and sparkle effects. It even defies gravity and can teleport to any player!

SHYFOOX

Shyfoox is a relative newcomer to making games in Roblox – not that it shows in Wolves' Life 2, or Shyfoox's other popular creations, Furana and Dragon's Life. Keep on reading to learn how Shyfoox studios first set out as a development group, their inspiration, and the effects of Roblox fame.

ON FIRST STEPS
Trying out new things isn't easy, as Shyfoox explains. "One day I just derped around on my computer and saw the Roblox Studio icon. I was like, 'What could be so hard?' and I opened it up and tried to make a road. It did not look like a road at all; I just copied and pasted bricks all around the place, unaware of the scale, move, and anchor tools. I was about to completely give up but my friend challenged me to compete with him to build something, and since I'd tried Studio before, I completely wrecked him! That is where I got my motivation to keep building."

ON UNEXPECTED INSPIRATION
"I remember once I woke up in the middle of the night and I felt this rush, and I knew the answer to a problem I'd had the day before!" says Shyfoox. "I often come up with ideas in the shower, at school, or in the middle of the night."

ON THE PERILS OF FAME
"I really miss being a normal player sometimes," Shyfoox confides. "I can't go in my own game without being crowded around. My fondest memory of Roblox is for sure the innocence I had before this."

ZOMBIE RUSH

Welcome to the zombie apocalypse. Your only mission in Zombie Rush is to endure the endless onslaught of the undead. Take your pick from dozens of weapons and go into the arena to see how long you and your crack squad of zombie killers can survive.

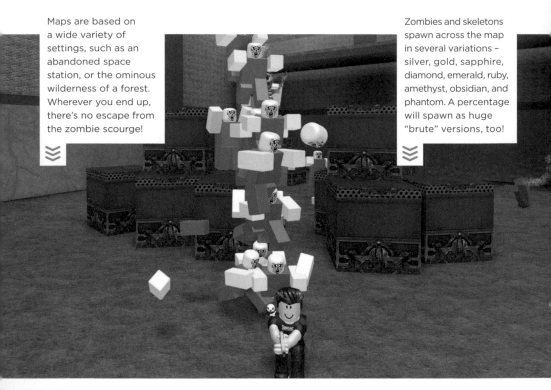

Maps are based on a wide variety of settings, such as an abandoned space station, or the ominous wilderness of a forest. Wherever you end up, there's no escape from the zombie scourge!

Zombies and skeletons spawn across the map in several variations – silver, gold, sapphire, diamond, emerald, ruby, amethyst, obsidian, and phantom. A percentage will spawn as huge "brute" versions, too!

Arm yourself with primary and secondary weapons on the weapon select screen. The primary is a ranged weapon, while the secondary is a close-combat melee piece. You unlock more powerful weapons as you level up.

GAME STATS

STUDIO:	Beacon Studio
SUBGENRES:	Horror, Shooter, Tycoon
VISITS:	
FAVORITED:	

QUICK TIPS

FISH IN A BARREL

If a swarm is chasing a fellow survivor, it can make getting kills and beating waves easier. Strafe beside the swarm and fire, aiming for normal zombies to maximize kills. Just beware that they may chase you instead!

REGENERATION

If your health is running low, stop going for the kill and start running away. Use sloped land and obstacles to slow pursuers down slightly. Allow your health to regenerate a bit before starting to attack again.

SWITCHING SIDES

If you don't want to wait for the next round to begin after a premature death, press the zombie button from the menu when you're in the lobby. This lets you play as the undead and makes life difficult for remaining players.

HIGH GROUND

Though these particular fiends can jump and reach high places, too, seeking elevated ground could buy you a bit of time in a pinch and let you thin out the herd from safety. Make sure that you don't get trapped with no way down.

HOMINGBEACON

When HomingBeacon was starting out as a game creator, he saw it as a way of earning expensive hats and game features, but then he realized that making them was really fun, too! Here he explains how a new game comes together, and the surprising origins of Zombie Rush's zombies.

ON PLANNING NEW UPDATES

"I rely on the community to help me fix my game and help pick my next update," he says. "If I notice a lot of suggestions for a certain feature in my messages then I try to make it happen."

ON STARTING GAMES

"I tend to start with the game type," says HomingBeacon. "I like looking at what could be done better and go from there. Staying motivated while working on the beginning of a project is the most difficult part, but after you have the framework done, it's pretty easy."

ON EFFECTIVE ZOMBIE RUSHING

His best advice for zombie hunters? "Constantly moving away from the zombies can keep you alive for longer, and aiming for headshots will do more damage to zombies as well!"

ON ... ROBOT RUSH?

Zombies are so important to Zombie Rush that they're in the title, and yet, as HomingBeacon confesses, "In the beginning of development, I was testing with robot models instead of zombies and they didn't even have animations for the first year!"

GALAXY

Establish an all-conquering empire in the depths of space! As you mine resources and trade them on the open market to amass a fortune, will you use diplomacy to secure your faction's power, or will you go to war and fight for it with a formidable fleet? In Galaxy, the choice is yours!

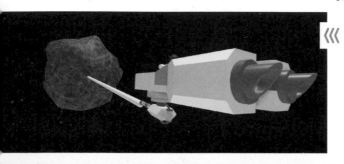

To begin with, spawn a mining ship and set course for an asteroid. Activate your mining lasers and wait for your cargo hold to fill.

Work together with your faction to take control of sectors that contain valuable ores. Defend your miners from enemy factions and alien attacks with your fast destroyers and powerful cruisers.

There are many ships to build, from efficient mining ships to powerful dreadnoughts, vast freighters, and carriers. To build them you'll need ores and credits.

Head back to a nearby station to sell the ores you mined. You can then buy more ores on the market to trade at other stations for higher prices.

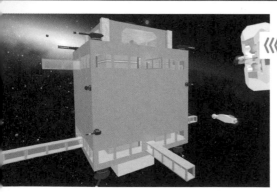

GAME STATS

DEVELOPER:	rcouret
SUBGENRES:	Sci-Fi, Trading, Simulation
VISITS:	
FAVORITED:	

QUICK TIPS

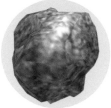   

MANIC MINER
The faction you belong to affects the price you'll get for your ores. Keep an eye on the Economy Matrix so you know which ores to mine for the most money, but remember some ores are only found in certain sectors.

ELITE TRADER
More expensive freighters hold more ore and are harder to destroy, so they're worth the expense. A sturdy ship can mean the difference between galactic domination and having your precious cargo stolen by looters!

DOGFIGHTER
Sometimes battles are unavoidable. Take note of the ship you're fighting against: if its guns are underneath, approach from above so they can't hit you. Keep your speed up to reduce the chance of shots hitting you.

FACTION CONTROL
You'll need powerful ships to bring down an enemy base, and it can mean losses to your fleet. Ally with other factions to increase your numbers – it's vital to work together and know the limitations of the ships on your side.

RCOURET

rcouret was an experienced programmer when he first signed up in 2013 to play with his son. When he saw Roblox Studio, he started to experiment with it and began a successful Roblox game development career. Let's hear how he started, gained inspiration, and created something amazing!

ON EXPERIENCE
When rcouret first discovered Roblox, he had already mastered multiple programming languages. "So learning Lua wasn't too difficult. I appreciated that Roblox handled most of the graphics for me and I could make the games that I'd always dreamed of."

ON DECONSTRUCTING GAMES
As he was learning Studio, rcouret noticed that Wingman8 had copy-unlocked his classic game Galleons. "I downloaded and studied it and I learned quite a few things about how it all fit

together and began making my first real game, Field of Battle, which eventually became a big hit," he says.

ON HIS BEST GALAXY MOMENT
"Both sides had several dreadnoughts and battleships valued at several million credits. The battle was intense and there were thousands of laser shots and missiles streaking through space. At some point I remembered that I created all of this from nothing more than a baseplate. It was great to know all of these players were having such a great time with my creation."

SHARD SEEKERS

You are a Shard Seeker, wanderer of a huge land of towns, mountains, lakes, and caverns. Valuable shards are raining down from the sky, and it's up to you to find them. With them, you can buy new characters to play as, or purchase pets, which unlock abilities from flight to fire-breathing!

Watch for shards' trails as they fall from the sky, then go collect them! Part of the challenge of the game is finding your way up to the plateaus where they lie.

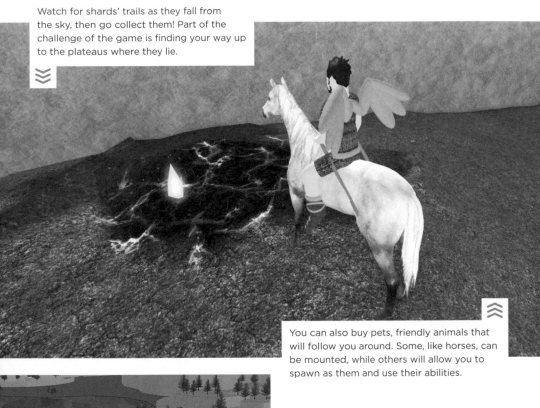

You can also buy pets, friendly animals that will follow you around. Some, like horses, can be mounted, while others will allow you to spawn as them and use their abilities.

You can use collected shards to buy new characters. You start the game as a human, but can buy the ability to assume the role of hobbits, orcs, elves, and more.

GAME STATS

DEVELOPER:	Tomarty
SUBGENRES:	RPG, Simulation
VISITS:	
FAVORITED:	

QUICK TIPS

LOOKING GOOD
Explore appearance customization options, including gender, skin color, and clothes, when you make a new character. Having a diverse character roster will expand the fun, especially if you intend on taking part in role-play.

SCALE MODEL
At a cost of 8,000 shards, the dragon is very expensive, but it can breathe fire, fly, and you can ride it! However, it's only half as expensive as the shadow dragon, which flies extremely fast. It's the ultimate shard-seeker's ride!

BALANCE BEAM
Often, the only way up to a platform is via a narrow beam, and if you fall, you'll have to trek all the way back up again! Use the run control to slow your speed enough to help you move more precisely and navigate tricky areas better.

DOUBLE TROUBLE
Your character has the ability to dual-wield! Set your sword in slot one and your pickaxe in slot two to increase your maximum damage output so you can face stronger enemies, like bears, on more equal terms.

TOMARTY

Having been introduced to programming by his father when he was eight years old, Tomarty has always made games on Roblox. Here he explains the magic behind the technology that runs Shard Seekers and why he's happy to take his time while realizing his ambitions.

ON PLAYING THE LONG GAME
Tomarty has plans to add lots of features, but won't rush. "I could add tons of new mechanics and items right now and get the game hyped up, but I want to take my time and do it right so it will last a very long time," he says. "It's ambitious, but I think my ultimate goal would be to make it as fleshed out as games like Skyrim."

ON NETWORKING MAGIC
Asked what he's most proud of in Shard Seekers, Tomarty says it's the way the game downloads as it's played, instead of all at once. "No joke,

Shard Seekers could support millions of unique animal types without impacting load times," he claims. "Now I plan to make Shard Seekers into Roblox's first truly 'massive' MMORPG."

ON MAKING A MAGIC SYSTEM
Planning features can be tricky. "I'm still very indecisive about what kinds of magic spells the game will have, and what the tiers of armor will be," Tomarty admits, but the sky's the limit. "The system is designed in an extremely powerful way, so players could dual-wield spells, or mix and match dual-wielded swords."

ULTIMATE DRIVING: WESTOVER ISLANDS

Buckle up for one of the most realistic driving simulators on Roblox! In Ultimate Driving: Westover Islands you'll hop in one of several dozen cars, negotiating realistic traffic lights, speed restrictions, and tolls along the way. You can even work a job while you're cruising around the highways.

Once you're familiar with the road you can buy game passes to take jobs. Police officers can arrest players who break road rules, firemen put out fires, and highway workers tow defunct vehicles.

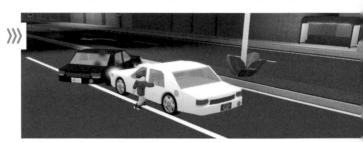

You begin with $10,000 to buy a starter car, but you can earn additional money simply by cruising around. Each car generates a different amount per mile. But drive carefully! You'll get fined if you're caught speeding.

Customize your car at body shops, where you can change its color and license plates, even adding your own text to them.

GAME STATS

DEVELOPER:	TwentyTwoPilots
SUBGENRES:	Town and City, Driving, Simulation
VISITS:	
FAVORITED:	

QUICK TIPS

CAR MECHANICS

As you drive your car, it will consume fuel. Fill it up with your fuel can, which you'll need to top off at gas stations. If you want to leave your car behind without it despawning, press the "park" button to prevent it from disappearing.

SEE THE SIGNS

Keep your eye on the road signs as you drive. They explain the speed limit of the road you're on, and warn you of upcoming hazards. Note that some highways will charge you tolls when you pass certain points, too.

BOUNTY HUNTER

As players rack up traffic offenses, they earn a bounty on their name, which police players will claim if they manage to catch them! How big a bounty can you carry before you're busted? How big a bounty can you reel in?

HOME FUN

There are myriad houses dotted across the Westover Islands, which are available to buy for $50,000. You can invite other players to be your housemates so they can enter your property whenever they like as well.

TWENTYTWOPILOTS

TwentyTwoPilots' combined interest in Roblox and cars started way back in 2008, when he played a demolition derby game. Since then he's mastered the art of the car sim, and veered between entries in his Ultimate Driving franchise. Read his take on creating worlds, businesses, and followings below.

ON MAP MAKING

Because the core of the UD series is essentially complete, each release is really about designing new maps. "Usually this starts out with my sketching a rough map, which fits like a puzzle piece into the Ultimate Driving universe. After that, I start building the map, usually starting at a border that's shared with an existing part of the universe."

ON PLAYER BASE SIZE

"From both a player and developer perspective, my favorite aspect of the community has

to be its sheer size," says TwentyTwoPilots. "As a developer, there's an endless supply of players who could potentially be playing on my creations. As a player, there's an endless amount of awesome games I can enjoy with friends."

ON A PROFITABLE PASSION

Making games in Roblox was initially just a creative outlet. "Then it became profitable! While the creativity is the core of why I do what I do, I never would've been able to pour so much time and effort into expressing it if it wasn't simultaneously helping me to earn a living."

WHATEVER FLOATS YOUR BOAT

Build a boat, survive a flood, and battle other players in this crazy, creative shooter! Design a boat on dry land at the beginning of each round and when the waters rise, it's all hands on deck as the battle begins. Take to your cannons, arm your pistols, and fight for naval supremacy!

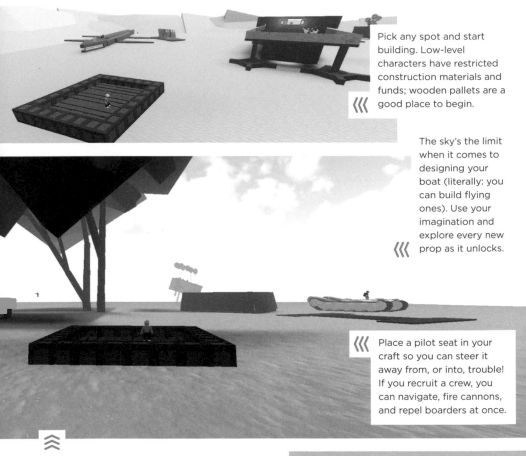

Pick any spot and start building. Low-level characters have restricted construction materials and funds; wooden pallets are a good place to begin.

The sky's the limit when it comes to designing your boat (literally: you can build flying ones). Use your imagination and explore every new prop as it unlocks.

Place a pilot seat in your craft so you can steer it away from, or into, trouble! If you recruit a crew, you can navigate, fire cannons, and repel boarders at once.

When the flood water rises you can fire your gun, swing your sword, and fire cannons. You'll earn XP for destroying props on enemy boats and money for KO'ing players.

GAME STATS

DEVELOPER:	Quenty
SUBGENRES:	Building, PvP, Shooter
VISITS:	
FAVORITED:	

QUICK TIPS

BALANCED LOAD
Whatever Floats Your Boat utilizes Roblox's physics to its fullest potential. If heavy armor plates and cannons are not distributed evenly, your boat is in danger of capsizing. Use lots of buoyant props to support it.

CASH BOX
Grab chests after the flood dries. They contain XP and money that will replenish your funds and allow you to rebuild your boat. Sometimes there'll be an equippable cannon, so you can deliver damage on the run.

CROW'S NEST
Keep an eye on the other players' boats as you construct your vessel and think about what disadvantages they have. If they're designing a tank, maybe you could build a ship that can outrun it and take quick shots at it.

SHOT PUT
A cannonball's trajectory drops over long distances. Aim high so you hit your target. And remember, you can use it to drop damage down on the open tops of your enemies' ships, ignoring their armored sides.

QUENTY

Quenty started making games on Roblox in 2009 at the tender age of 12, and hasn't stopped since. To share all that experience, he's made some of his code open source, so anyone can use it! Here he shares his thoughts on coding instead of doing homework, and problems with big boats.

ON FAILING
Quenty admires anyone learning how to make games. "They don't know how to program, or design a fun game, but they're going to try and fail dozens of times. And someday they'll succeed in making something great."

ON LATE NIGHTS
Quenty's fondest Roblox memories are of staying up at night. "I'd convince my parents I had homework to do, then stay up until 2 or 3 a.m., building on Roblox." He'd play on servers with friends and rig all their creations to explode.

"The night always ended with us pushing Roblox to the limit and crashing the server."

ON PROBLEMS WITH BIG BOATS
"There was this issue in my game where players built big boats and used them to fling enemy boats off the map with physics. So I added a mechanic where fallen boats get back their money, so the players can rebuild. Other players found this out and built a boat underneath the map, then repeatedly spawned more to farm experience. I wanted my game to encourage creativity and learning. It worked."

AFTER THE FLASH: DEEP SIX

Step into post-armageddon Georgia, U.S.A. and play out life as a survivor in the lawless world that a nuclear apocalypse has left behind.
This richly drawn world of factions competing for territory across a large and detailed map is designed for you to create your own stories.

Spawn at a location where your character would live. There's a huge amount to see in this detailed world; explore and meet other players and get to know their characters.

Read the lore behind the game, and imagine a character who might live there. What faction would they join? What would they think, say, and do?

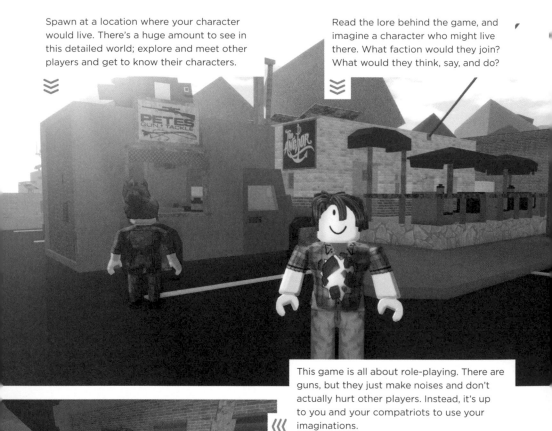

This game is all about role-playing. There are guns, but they just make noises and don't actually hurt other players. Instead, it's up to you and your compatriots to use your imaginations.

GAME STATS

STUDIO:	After The Flash Advisory Board
SUBGENRES:	RPG, Exploration
VISITS:	
FAVORITED:	

QUICK TIPS

RULE ONE
Since you're role-playing, take care to avoid acting in unnatural ways. Play it as if it's the real world – don't jump off things that no one could survive, and don't pretend you've survived a point-blank shot!

RADIO TUNE
Listen to the radio! Apart from playing great music, the DJ also brings the world to life with details about the events that shaped it. You could use these to inspire your character's personality, or begin a new adventure.

FIRST ENCOUNTER
When you come across a group of other players, be careful not to cut into their role-play. You might accidentally mess up their story! Take the time to listen to them and see how you can fit in as a stranger.

TOP CHAT
Use speech marks in chat to show when your character is talking, and use asterisks to show when you're performing actions, such as giving food to someone. Make sure you listen to others as much as you talk.

CHADTHECREATOR

In addition to the After the Flash series, which kicked off back in 2011, ChadTheCreator has made many other kinds of games in Roblox. Here he talks about how he looks to his players for inspiration, and how he found making Roblox games a natural progression from making board games.

ON WHY HE MAKES GAMES
ChadTheCreator finds making games an "incredibly engaging process," and he's been doing it for a long time. "I made board games and card games when I was younger," he says. "Roblox felt like the natural, virtual extension of game development that I'd been looking for. Seeing people enjoying a game you made is one of the best feelings."

ON HIS FONDEST ROBLOX MEMORY
"Some friends and I went into a building game and made giant rockets to blast the whole server's population into space," he remembers. "We had a lot fun organizing the engine mechanics and designing oddball ships."

ON TAKING IN PLAYERS' IDEAS
"I take community suggestions into account," he says. "Many core parts of my games originally came from player suggestions and feedback."

ON ENDING DEEP SIX
He reveals he's planning an ending to this particular episode, which will be based on "how I observe the players interact in-game."

PINEWOOD COMPUTER CORE

Explore a secret underground facility that's about to explode! Your mission is to keep a supercomputer from overheating, but you'll likely be distracted by something else entirely. Explore every corner of the facility, press every button, discover secrets, and you may make it out alive!

The core room features status readouts for the computer's coolant systems. Use them to monitor its heat levels and to plan what you should do next.

Work as a team to reach the sectors where you'll find the controls for the systems that will keep the core cool.

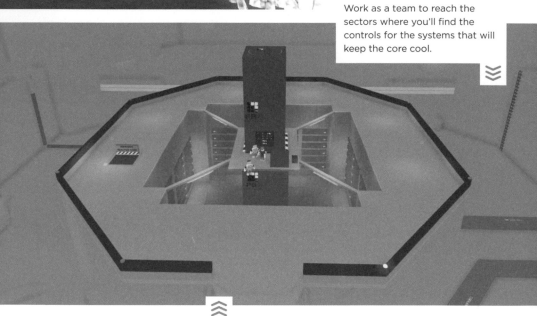

If you can't keep the core from melting down, you'll have three minutes to evacuate to the launch silos or the exit elevator to the surface.

GAME STATS

DEVELOPER: Diddleshot

SUBGENRES: Sci-Fi, RPG, Exploration

VISITS:

FAVORITED:

QUICK TIPS

WALKABOUT
The Pinewood Computer Core is a huge facility and there's lots to see and do aside from keeping the computer running. Use a truck to get around; you can respawn them by touching the purple floor plates.

GEAR UP
The radiation levels of the computer's internal core are so high that you'll need a protective hazmat suit to enter. However, if the core is overheating, even the suit won't be able to withstand radiation, and you'll be unable to enter.

SECRET NUMBER
At the mainframe of the core, there's a keypad, which, if you know the code, will lead to a second keypad. If you happen to also know the second code, it will lead the way to a third keypad! Few know what lies behind it ...

GOING UP
The computer core is only part of the whole Pinewood installation. You can also travel up to the surface to explore Pinewood Research Facility. It's a separate game that will load when you board the correct elevator.

DIDDLESHOT

Diddleshot's first game was a dog food factory, which involved moving things around with conveyor belts. His second was about destroying trains. Then came his games about driving huge mining vehicles and tumbling around in washing machines – you get the idea: he loves playing with physics!

ON THE FUN OF PHYSICS
Physics were part of one of Diddleshot's formative Roblox moments. "One of my fondest memories was blowing up the classic Roblox HQ when I first started in 2008. The physics and everything really enticed and fascinated me. I wanted to make and play more!"

ON DEVELOPMENT SATISFACTION
"When I created a game and lots of people played it for the first time, I realized people could enjoy what I create," Diddleshot says. "Being able to create something big and

interesting that people ultimately enjoy, then improving it further, gives me great satisfaction."

ON THE BEST SOURCE OF IDEAS
"I always take ideas from the community because not only are they the ones playing and getting involved in my games, but they also have some of the best ideas," says Diddleshot. "I write them down on a notepad, ready to check them out when I get into working on the games."

ON THE BIG COMPUTER CORE SECRET ...
"The third code is a lie."

MINER'S HAVEN

Have you ever wanted to generate a fortune so huge you'll have trouble comprehending the numbers? Then you've got the right game! Place droppers, conveyors, and upgraders freely to create a unique mine. When you're done, destroy it all to be reborn with even more powerful items.

<<< You start on the plot of land on which you'll build your mine. It will have an iron dropper, a conveyor belt, and a furnace already built. You'll need to move them around before they start making any money for you!

Spend money in the shop to buy new iron droppers, and upgrade to silver ones and higher when you can. Place upgraders to increase each ore's value.

Steadily build up your mine as your funds increase. It will keep generating ores even when you aren't playing! Unlock new items with your mounting riches and explore the world!

GAME STATS

STUDIO:	berezaa Games
SUBGENRES:	Building, Tycoon, Exploration
VISITS:	
FAVORITED:	

QUICK TIPS

CASH INJECTION

Most upgraders have a limit on the value that they can add to your ore, so bear this in mind when making a chain of them. Upgraders that aren't adding value to ores are taking up valuable money-making space!

MOVE IT

Try out the many conveyor belt variations, which can be used to build complex systems to collect, upgrade, and smelt ores. Make use of the different designs to create systems that will serve multiple droppers at once.

SCIENCE TIME

Some powerful items can only be bought with Research Points. You can earn them by finding boxes that appear randomly in the land around your mine and also by building certain items that generate them.

BACK TO LIFE

When you've earned $25 quintillion (a seriously large amount of money!) you can be reborn. Your mine will be destroyed and you'll only keep your high-tier items, but you'll get a reborn-tier item and become even stronger!

BEREZAA

berezaa's games are deep and technically complex, and the systems allow a degree of exploration and experimentation. They're qualities that he tries to instill in games from the outset. Here he explains why creativity is so important, and why he makes games, even though he doesn't like coding!

ON NOT BEING A NATURAL CODER

"I know a lot of other kids who love coding, but that isn't me," he says. "When I found Roblox, it seemed like a dream come true – a physics engine where you can create anything. So I made bases and towns, and somewhere along the line, I realized I wanted to create a game. I pushed myself to learn the skills I needed to make my dreams a reality."

ON THE DIFFICULTY OF MAKING GAMES

"It's the part between coming up with an awesome idea and finishing that idea," he explains. "There are times when you doubt yourself. Some tasks feel impossible, bugs and issues come up that seem hopeless to solve. But you just have to push through it. You have to remember what you're doing this for and see it to completion."

ON THE VALUE OF PLAYER CREATIVITY

"I'm proud of how much creative control my game grants players," berezaa says. "It pushes them to think outside the box. Building games are where I got my inspiration, so I hope that my games can pass the torch to future creators."

HIDE AND SEEK EXTREME

You've played this in the real world, but never on this scale! Hide and Seek Extreme shrinks players to the size of mice and lets them loose in giant levels based on an average house. As a hider, you'll be searching for the perfect place to stay out of sight, and as "It," you'll be finding them.

The game randomly selects a map and the player who will be It. The longer you play and the more success you have, the more chance it'll be you.

If you're It, you have four minutes to find the hiders to eliminate them from the game! You move faster than the hiding players, and can use a special ability!

Use jump-pads to get on to tables and chairs, and look for purple pads which will teleport you to distant locations. Explore everywhere to become the best hider and seeker.

If you're a hider, you have a minute to find a hiding place before whoever is It is able to move and search for you. Look for somewhere you can't be found easily, and keep out of sight!

GAME STATS

DEVELOPER:	Tim7775
SUBGENRES:	PvP, Exploration
VISITS:	
FAVORITED:	

QUICK TIPS

SPECIAL POWERS

When you're It and playing as one of the default characters, you can put down glue to stop hiders in their tracks. Other It characters can sprint, or put down cameras to watch out for hiders in multiple areas.

HUNTER'S EYE

As a hider, Spectate view is your secret weapon. It allows you to watch anyone who's It as they run around, giving you time to escape if they're heading toward you. You may also pick up some better hiding places!

IN PLAIN SIGHT

The best hiding places can be out in the open. Choose a chair leg (or similar) and watch It closely, making sure you move around the leg to stay out of sight. They'll never guess you'd hide somewhere so blatantly obvious.

STORE CREDIT

Earn credits by surviving rounds and catching hiders, and also by collecting coins from the maps. Buy new It characters with them so you can use their special abilities, pets, and taunts to drive your rivals crazy!

TIM7775

Getting to watch the quality of both Roblox and its games increase since he began using the platform in 2009 has been a favorite part of Roblox for Tim7775. Here he reveals the secret to how he starts designing a hit game, and shares a tip for being a top hider.

ON ROBLOX'S USP

Tim7775 likes Roblox because it deals with lots of difficult things about making games. "Getting a cross-platform multiplayer game running in a few minutes is unique to Roblox," he says. "This allows game developers to focus more on making the gameplay fun instead of solving difficult technical issues."

ON FINISHING UP

"In my eyes, the hardest part of making a game is finishing it. Most games fall apart due to failing to identify the scope of the project when starting, and increasing that scope during development." This is known as "feature creep." "Common advice in the game industry is to start with a minimum viable product."

ON MINIMUM VIABLE PRODUCTS

"I start all my games by creating a minimum viable product based on a gameplay mechanic," says Tim7775. "It's the simplest game you can make while still having the core gameplay in place. I then get people to test the game and gather feedback on whether it's engaging or not. If it is, I develop it further."

FLOOD ESCAPE

Take the ultimate test of agility as you escape a sinking facility. In Flood Escape you'll use all your parkour skills to beat the rising water and find an exit. The challenges keep coming, though, as you choose different skill levels and modes to keep the flooding fresh.

From the spawn point, enter the training area to learn the basics, or go straight to the easy or medium elevators to jump in and join a multiplayer game.

You need to jump on the platforms to get to the exit gate above. To open it, each of the blue buttons must be touched. Be quick! Water will begin to rise and if you fall in, it's game over.

If you can survive four rooms, your final challenge is to solve a puzzle. Press the buttons on each side of the door to find the pattern that turns their light green.

GAME STATS

DEVELOPER:	Crazyblox
SUBGENRES:	Escape, Obby
VISITS:	
FAVORITED:	

QUICK TIPS

PUSH BUTTON

If you press six of the cube-shaped buttons as you beat the flooding rooms, you'll play a bonus round after completing the combination lock challenge. It's a surprise timed puzzle that will earn you yet more points.

CODE BREAKER

Solve the button combination puzzle by trying out patterns in a logical sequence. If someone else is working on it, be careful not to disrupt their careful process. If they fail, everyone in the round will fail!

POINTS = PRIZES

Wins earn you access to Extreme mode and special abilities, while points for completing rooms and solving puzzles will buy aesthetic items and access to Flood Gauntlet, a PvP area in which you battle with Flood Swords.

SIMON SAYS

If you've gotten it wrong and seem to be stranded, don't forget that you can climb on many objects. And when you don't know where to go next, watch the other players. They'll often show you the way up to the gate.

CRAZYBLOX

From exploring level editors and game engines, Crazyblox always knew he wanted to make games, but the accessibility of Studio and its online features put him on the path to becoming a Roblox creator. Here he explains why it's hard to keep to one idea, and why listening to the community is vital.

ON FOCUSING

"The most difficult thing for me is to stick to one project and solely focus on that," Crazyblox explains. He'd often jump between different ideas. "While it was great for practice and getting experience, I never really had a big game to show all of my work. I still mess with other smaller projects as a breather if I burn out on working on my main games."

ON EVALUATING IDEAS

The community is valuable for testing Crazyblox's ideas. "It's super-important to gather feedback from people who play and test your games, because they are the ones who ultimately decide if your game makes it big!"

ON REINVENTING THE ... WATER?

Crazyblox is very proud of the swimming mechanic in his next game, Flood Escape 2. "I would've used the terrain's own water system but it didn't offer the fidelity and dynamics I was after. I wanted smooth, adjustable heights and more accessible controls for the player. The fact that I'm able to design my own underwater system shows how capable Roblox can be."

CAR CRUSHERS

Car Crushers is your opportunity to cause carnage. Choose from cars, trucks, buses, and much more, then drive them into your choice of crusher to squash, spike, collide, and smash them to smithereens! The more you destroy, the more money you'll earn to unlock even better cars to crush.

You start in the showroom, home to dozens of very stylish, very crushable vehicles. The points around the edge are where you spawn each car. To begin with, choose one of two free vehicles to crush.

Time to smash! Drive it on to the conveyor belt of a smasher and jump out. When you're at a safe distance, hit the button to start the destruction.

The car's value is the most money you can earn when you crush it. The more money you have, the more valuable cars you get to crush, up to the Mirari Electrica, worth a billion dollars! After crushing, hit the "Teleport to Spawn" button to return to the showroom and pick another car to smash.

GAME STATS

DEVELOPER:	Panwellz
SUBGENRES:	Town and City, Driving, Tycoon
VISITS:	
FAVORITED:	

QUICK TIPS

QUICK CASH
To make money quickly, always crush the most valuable car you are able to spawn so you're earning maximum money. Don't worry, you don't spend money to spawn cars. Your rising balance just unlocks new vehicles.

SMASH SMART
To get the most out of each crush, pick a smasher that will do the most damage to your car. Roof Lasers might not work on a low car, for example. The most efficient is the Giant Crusher, but that often means it has a long queue.

BODY PARTS
Watch that you don't lose your head when you're crushing! Stand too close to the speeding train smasher and you might lose a body part! Don't worry, if you do get maimed, you'll respawn in the showroom again.

SECRET SMASHER
There are some secrets to find around this strange island of smashing machines if you explore it closely. For example, can you find the Energy Core? Investigate the areas around each crusher to see if you can find it.

PANWELLZ

Panwellz steadily built up his experience with making games, slowly developing his skills through little updates and remakes. Here, he explains what attracts him to making games, why it's important to attract players to his creations, and divulges a little secret to a big bang!

ON SHARING
The thing that got Panwellz hooked on game development was connecting with other players. "I could make something I cared about and have other people play and take part in the work I had done," he says.

ON PLAYER RETENTION
You might think that programming and bugs are the biggest challenge for a game developer, but for Panwellz, it's getting players to come back to play again that challenges him most. "You can work really hard on a game and put effort into every detail, but if the gameplay isn't fun or any other part of the design is flawed it won't get very far."

ON ESCAPING A MELTDOWN
There's a secret Energy Core that can turn Car Crushers into a more dramatic affair. "If you encounter a meltdown, which causes an explosion that destroys everything, then quickly spawn a car, drive outside the building, look for a big white beam in the sky and drive toward it to get to an escape helicopter and survive the explosion." Now you know how to survive!

FANTASTIC FRONTIER

Venture into lands of legend in Fantastic Frontier, an RPG in which you'll battle monsters, find valuable loot, and complete epic quests! You'll make this detailed fantasy world your own as you collect powerful weapons and armor, learn clever magic, and procure houses in bustling towns.

You start with a simple wooden sword, so try not to get into too many fights. Pick mushrooms and flowers to sell to Big Box in the town square and earn gold.

There's lots to discover in Topple Town's shops and side alleys. Smart early investments include a pickaxe to mine ores, and a new sword from Reus the Smith.

The most valuable items are found farther into the world. As you buy better equipment, you'll be able to face the dangerous monsters that inhabit it.

Eat food to partially regain health, or fully heal by resting at the inn for 200 gold. If you buy a house, you can rest for free!

GAME STATS

DEVELOPER:	Spectrabox
SUBGENRES:	RPG, Exploration
VISITS:	
FAVORITED:	

QUICK TIPS

DEAD RECKONING
When you die, you'll lose all the items in your inventory except your equipment and a portion of your gold. Keep your health up, and make sure your equipment can withstand any threats you're likely to encounter!

GOLD RUSH
Feeling brave? Make fast money by paying Captain Finnegan to take you to the Town of Right and Wrong. The monsters may be tougher than you've encountered, but the plants you collect there are very valuable.

METTLE TEST
Some areas of the world are home to players who prey on the unready, such as Frigid Waste. Visit these PVP-enabled areas at your own peril ... or take the opportunity to challenge other players in a battle to the death!

ENERGY DROP
Sprinting and swinging your sword consumes stamina. If you run out, you won't be able to continue until it recharges, which can be the difference between victory and death if you're in the middle of a fight.

SPECTRABOX

It took Spectrabox, working with his brother, just 10 months to release Fantastic Frontier. They'd only made simple games before, if they even finished them at all, yet Fantastic Frontier is a huge and detailed world. Here, Spectrabox explains the value of staying organized and why engine updates are fun.

ON MAKING A BIG WORLD
"I like the world we made in Fantastic Frontier and how full of life it feels," Spectrabox tells us. "The map is pretty big, and I think for its size the density of content and detail makes it feel very alive. It's fun just exploring the world; there are always surprises."

ON STAYING ORGANIZED
"For me, the most difficult aspect of game development is keeping everything organized. In large games, there are tons of moving parts that need to work with each other." Spectrabox's solution is lots of planning. "There are always things you have to do that you didn't plan for. If your game is not well-organized, adding even a simple feature can be a nightmare!"

ON ROBLOX'S EVOLUTION
Spectrabox loves watching the Roblox community respond to the Roblox engine as it's updated. "Any time a new feature is released it is great to see it put to use in new and unique ways and watch the games evolve. There are so many games on Roblox now that would have been impossible to create just a few years ago."

ROBLOX TITANIC

Experience the events of April 15, 1912, when the RMS Titanic collided with an iceberg on its maiden voyage and sank. Explore a re-creation of the ship that was meant to be unsinkable with up to 40 other players, try to change the course of history, or simply role-play the fateful evening.

))) You board the ship from a lobby. Each door leads to a different part of the ship, but as they're submerged, they'll begin to lock ...

Follow the ship's inexorable demise as it takes on water on the lowest decks and begins to list to one side. Eventually the entire vessel will break up!)))

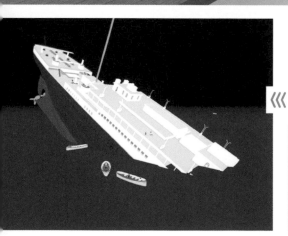

You'll earn Risk as you get closer to the water, which can be spent on Hax – visual effects that can turn the game black and white, for example – or on (((special equippable items.

GAME STATS

STUDIO:	Virtual Valley Games
SUBGENRES:	Survival, Exploration
VISITS:	
FAVORITED:	

QUICK TIPS

DECK INSPECTOR
The in-game Titanic has been lovingly modeled on its real-life counterpart, so there's lots to see, from the engine room and the bridge to first class and its famous grand staircase. But tour them before they begin to flood!

ROLE PLAY
You can pick a name and occupation to display above your head so you can act out the sinking with your friends. You can also vote to experience a historically accurate sinking or one that's based on the popular movie.

RUSH FOR EXIT
As you stay close to the waterline on the lower deck, you might find your route up to safer ground is blocked. And when you're on the top deck, be careful not to fall as the ship breaks up. Don't say you weren't warned!

SAIL AWAY
There are several lifeboats on board the ship, which only paid crew members are able to set up. But once they've been let loose, you can risk swimming out to them. Make sure you don't stay in the water for too long though.

THEAMAZEMAN

Having been part of the community since September 2008, TheAmazeman enjoyed the early days of Roblox when its most popular genres were first being formed. Here, he explains what keeps him on the platform, and what it means to be a captain going down with his ship.

ON SHIPBUILDING
"In Roblox Titanic, I am most proud of the equations I devised to sink the ship, along with the team I assembled that built it."

ON GOING DOWN WITH THE SHIP
Here's something you might not know about playing with the Captain Game Pass on Roblox Titanic: "Because you get 9001 health, if you go into the captain's room when water starts flooding, you would survive for almost the rest of the round, from the bridge flooding, past the ship splitting into two, and the final plunge. The saying is 'a captain goes down with his ship,' and this huge amount of health allows the player to play that exact role!"

ON HURDLES IN GAME CREATION
Obstacles in game development are often in your head: "The most difficult thing is getting past mental hurdles of things you don't believe you can solve due to lack of knowledge and experience. It forces you to learn, which is good, but sometimes it can go on for days or weeks and they often result in starting new projects entirely, abandoning the problem altogether."

MAD PAINTBALL 2

Two teams face off in this intense paintball shooter. You'll play three game modes, King of the Hill, Capture the Flag, and Domination on the detailed Tranquility 2 map, and bring to bear four powerful weapons against your opponents. This is first-person Roblox paintballing at its best!

You'll start in the player setup screen. Equip a weapon to take into battle and select "DEPLOY." Note the game mode you'll be playing this round.

In King of the Hill, fight to hold an area. In CTF, capture the opposition's flag and take it to your base. In Domination, capture and hold three zones.

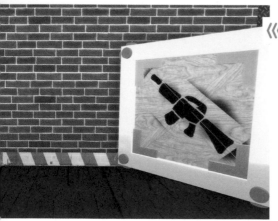

When you level up by winning games and defeating other players, you'll be awarded Rubies. Spend them on weapons, skin, and clothes crates from the shop, or additional inventory slots.

GAME STATS

STUDIO:	MAD STUDIO
SUBGENRES:	FPS, PvP
VISITS:	
FAVORITED:	

QUICK TIPS

RIGHT TOOL
The sniper is all about long-range, while the rifle is deadly accurate. The heavy's extended magazine is good for covering choke points where enemies gather. The powerful shotgun is for close-range engagements.

NEW PLAN
If your tactic isn't working and you keep getting defeated, change it! Take a different route, attack a different target, or use a different weapon. Keep the enemy guessing and you'll find much better luck.

SQUAD GOAL
Remember you're playing in a team and that you have an objective. Don't go for personal glory and attack the enemy head-on. Make sure you're capturing points and supporting the flag-carrier so everyone benefits.

SURE SHOT
Always aim down the sniper's sights and wait a moment for it to charge up before taking your shot. When you hear the beep, you'll deliver the most damage. But even a partially charged headshot should defeat an enemy.

LOLERIS

loleris is the lead developer of Mad Studio, the prolific development group behind Mad Paintball 2, so he not only makes games but manages a team as well! Read on for his wisdom on how to start making a new game, and how he's found Roblox to be a source of new friends.

ON STARTING
When loleris started out, he began by creating gameplay mechanics, but now they come last. "Now the first thing I do is spend a good while writing the game concept on paper, then working on data managing, menus and interfaces, and leave gameplay until the end."

ON MAKING NEW THINGS
"The most difficult thing is always trying to make something you've never tried to make before," loleris tells us. "Developers who want to be successful do that every day."

ON SHARING THE LOAD
"Lots of people think I don't do much when making my own games and only hire people to do it all," he says. But he certainly keeps busy, despite enlisting others to make maps and graphics. "I make templates for the maps and do all the scripting."

ON FINDING NEW FRIENDS
"I started making games to find more friends," he says. "When I made games that players found interesting, more people played them and I grew a community of people who liked what I make!"

WORLD EXPEDITION

Travel the world without leaving your seat! In World Expedition you can fly to eight of the world's most fascinating destinations to tour their sights. This is your chance to soak up the atmosphere of locations including Tokyo Tower and the Taj Mahal, and to discover their secrets.

Inside Roblox International Airport you'll find the departure board. Choose where you want to go, note the gate it leaves from, and get a boarding pass from a staff member. Find the correct gate and board your plane. »»

Once you've arrived at your destination, you're free to explore. Take a look at everything, go inside every building, and discover every corner of these exciting locations. «««

Buy souvenirs such as T-shirts to remember your visit, and read facts and other details about your destination by using the buttons on the left of the screen. «««

GAME STATS

DEVELOPER:	legoseed
SUBGENRES:	Exploration, Showcase
VISITS:	
FAVORITED:	

QUICK TIPS

EGG HUNT
There are many eggs carefully hidden around the locations for you to find. Touch them to collect them and you'll be rewarded with a Badge for each one. Can you find them all?

NEXT DESTINATION
In Lijiang, talk to a man at the end of the street, who will let you take a chair lift to the Great Wall of China. In Tokyo, you can take an elevator to the top of Tokyo Tower to view the landscape.

STREET TALK
Talk to street vendors to try their food. You could be sipping drinks and eating dim sum in the evening sun. And don't worry, it doesn't cost Robux or any other tokens, so go wild!

QUICK STOP
When you want to leave, you can save yourself the long walk back to the exit by resetting your character so you respawn at the location entrance, ready to fly back to Roblox International.

LEGOSEED

legoseed first discovered and played Roblox at the grand old age of 10, and has been, in his words, "messing around in it ever since." Here he explains his unique interest in eggs, the value of traveling in games, and his globe-dominating ambitions for World Expedition!

ON HUNTING EGGS
Ever wonder why you can find eggs in World Expedition? Well, it's down to legoseed's favorite memory of Roblox, which was the Egg Drop in 2010. "I was twelve years old and woke up at 5 a.m. to hunt eggs," he remembers. "It was so surreal and peaceful."

ON DISAPPOINTMENT
It's hard to please everyone all the time, and that can be difficult to deal with. "The most difficult part of development is facing players who are disappointed with your game," he says. "I try too hard to make everyone happy and it's discouraging when they're dissatisfied."

ON BROADENING HORIZONS
legoseed is proud of the experience World Expedition can give players of places outside their knowledge. "Where I'm from, geography gets glossed over in school," he says. "It's a very important thing to understand other cultures and walks of life besides your own."

ON BUILDING THE WORLD
legoseed's work on World Expedition has only just begun, having completed only 8 of 195 countries so far. Yes, he really does aim to do them all. "The next steps would be to create any of the remaining countries. Right now, I'm working on Morocco, Iceland, and Jamaica."

THE NORMAL ELEVATOR

It's just a normal elevator, right? Not quite! In The Normal Elevator, you'll take the strangest ride of your life. You won't know what to expect when the doors open – from a parkour challenge to a chicken-eating competition, and from a dancing cat to a ravenous dinosaur. How far can you go?

To begin your ride, simply walk across the lobby and step into the open elevator. You'll join other players and the doors will close, ready to bounce between floors.

Many stops are harmless minigames or scenes to watch, but others might kill you if you're not careful, sending you back to the lobby.

You'll be awarded a token at each stop. Save 10 tokens to buy food from the shop menu; each one has a different odd effect on your body!

GAME STATS

DEVELOPER:	NowDoTheHarlemShake
SUBGENRES:	Minigames, Humor
VISITS:	
FAVORITED:	

QUICK TIPS

SURVIVAL RIDE
Often, the things that can kill you come from the middle of the elevator doors, so keep away from the entrance and stay to the sides. But not always: listen for hints for what will happen next.

LAST STOP
Take a look at the leaderboard in the lobby to check how many elevator stops you've been on! Don't worry when you die on a run, though, as each stop will still be counted toward your total.

MEDAL MAKER
Some badges require you take part in activities, like the chicken-eating contest, but not everyone gets the opportunity to play. Raise the chance of being picked by buying The Chosen One Pass.

HAVE FUN
There are some big challenges in this game, like its parkour run, which you must complete before the elevator leaves. But winning doesn't matter, and neither does dying! The most important thing is to have fun.

NOWDOTHEHARLEMSHAKE

It was five years before NowDoTheHarlemShake could understand scripting in Roblox, and then he made one of its most popular games. Here he explains how he accidentally released The Normal Elevator before it was finished, and how to have the most lifting experience while playing it.

ON THE BEST WAY TO PLAY
Riding an elevator isn't the hardest thing in the world, but NowDoTheHarlemShake has a tip to make it more fun. "Have you ever been stuck in an awkward elevator ride with people where it's dead silent, and then someone farts a little and it's even more awkward? Possibly not, but you can make the elevator ride fun by talking with other players. Tell them your random thoughts, make new friends!"

ON HOW NOT TO RELEASE A GAME
NowDoTheHarlemShake didn't quite mean to release The Normal Elevator when he did. After showing it to his friend Dapale, who helped make it, the pair went off to play something else. "I had forgotten to close the place, and after playing games for a few hours I came back to see my game had a few hundred players on it," he remembers. "I stayed up all night watching the player count go up and up, and then saw it become the number one popular game! I didn't add everything I wanted to before I released, but I did updates for it every night or so with help from Dapale to add new gameplay and fix bugs. I'd say it worked out pretty well." So there you have it – one of the most popular games on Roblox began as a happy accident.

MINING INC!

Work together to run a mine in Mining INC! You'll be digging deep to excavate precious minerals, hauling them out to the refinery and loading the refined product onto a ship. Buy new vehicles so you can work faster, but remember — the best miners are those who work as a team!

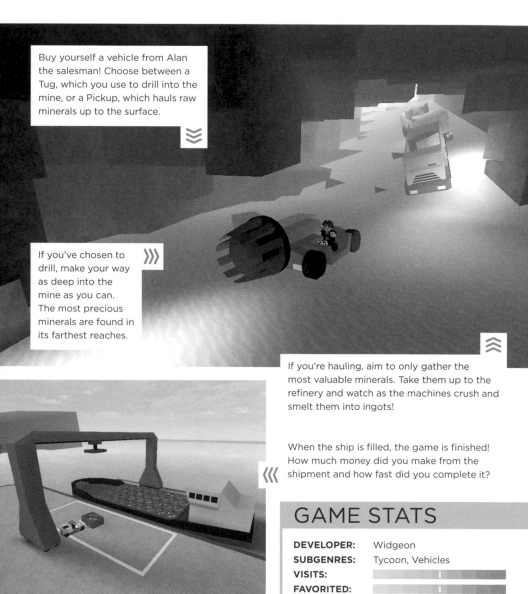

Buy yourself a vehicle from Alan the salesman! Choose between a Tug, which you use to drill into the mine, or a Pickup, which hauls raw minerals up to the surface.

If you've chosen to drill, make your way as deep into the mine as you can. The most precious minerals are found in its farthest reaches.

If you're hauling, aim to only gather the most valuable minerals. Take them up to the refinery and watch as the machines crush and smelt them into ingots!

When the ship is filled, the game is finished! How much money did you make from the shipment and how fast did you complete it?

GAME STATS

DEVELOPER:	Widgeon
SUBGENRES:	Tycoon, Vehicles
VISITS:	
FAVORITED:	

QUICK TIPS

TEAMWORK
The best mines are run by tight teams. Split labor between those excavating the mine, haulers who take minerals up to the refinery, and forklift drivers who drop finished crates at the ship.

PRECIOUS LOAD
Refine the most valuable minerals, to maximize the money you earn from each load. Consult the price list outside W&U Trucks; the most valuable ores are found deeper in the mine.

ROCK CHART
Use the map to find out where other members of your team are and where to find loose minerals to haul out of the mine. It's a great resource for coordinating your team's efforts.

TRUCK UP
As you earn money, invest it in buying newer and better trucks, which can carry more minerals and mine out more rock, then upgrade them to make them even faster and more effective.

WIDGEON

After being bitten by the Roblox bug playing Miked's Paintball all the way back in 2008, Widgeon began making things in Roblox Studio for himself. Here he tells us about what turned him from a gamer into a creator, the benefits of the platform, and what he wishes he'd made himself.

ON WHERE HE GOT STARTED
For his first game, Widgeon dragged some free plane models into an empty world and got 20 people to role-play a transportation company by flying planes between points in it. "That was my first realization that made me go, 'Oh wow, people like what I made!'" he says.

ON WHY HE USES ROBLOX
Roblox's big appeal to Widgeon is all its developer features. "Most of the hard work is done for you, including server hosting, a big community of players, good dev tools and APIs, so you can just click 'publish' and boom – it's on every platform Roblox supports!"

ON THE ROBLOX COMMUNITY
Widgeon is well-known in the Roblox community and hopes that he and his games can reach a wide audience. "Knowing I can make a positive impact on their lives, whether it's through my games or talking to players directly, is my favorite aspect of being part of it," he adds.

ON THE GAME HE WISHES HE'D MADE
Widgeon greatly admires Cleaning Simulator by creator zKevin, but he's being very hard on himself when he says, "I'll never have that much creativity." Look at all his works and you'll see he has creativity to spare! However, that leads us neatly into our next game ...

CLEANING SIMULATOR

Do you dream of experiencing the fun of cleaning with none of the elbow grease? That's what Cleaning Simulator is all about, plus a whole lot more silliness on the side. But beware: the strange corporation you're working for is not quite what it seems ... Only you can clean up this messy mystery!

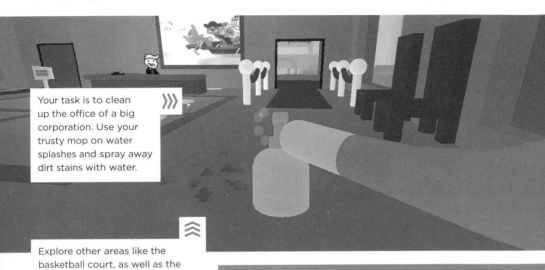

Your task is to clean up the office of a big corporation. Use your trusty mop on water splashes and spray away dirt stains with water.

Explore other areas like the basketball court, as well as the main building. Grab anything that can move, from doors to toilet seats, to see what's inside.

You refill the water spray from buckets around the level. There aren't many in the office building, so plan your work carefully.

Tapes are hidden everywhere! Carry the tape player to them and they'll play while you work. They are extremely silly.

GAME STATS

STUDIO:	BRIBBLECO
SUBGENRES:	Humor, Cleaning, Simulation
VISITS:	
FAVORITED:	

QUICK TIPS

EASTER EGGS
Cleaning Simulator is filled with secrets and jokes! Check out the desktop at the start of the game and open some of its folders. Look behind things, under things, and around things, and talk to everyone.

TOOL CARE
Keeping your mop and spray close as you clean is tricky. Try throwing them around instead of carrying them, and press the button outside the office to reveal them if you lose sight of them.

ROLL OUT
Remember that you can roll by double-tapping jump. It's not very maneuverable, but it's great for crossing long, flat distances quickly and for rolling down steep slopes.

GOOD SPORT
Cleaning isn't the only thing you can play. You and a friend can play hockey on one of the upper floors of the office, and you can go bowling, using your avatar to knock down pins.

ZKEVIN

zKevin led the development of Cleaning Simulator and is most inspired by seeing players' reactions to what he makes. Here he tells us about how being bad at making games is no hindrance to his creativity, and why giving games a good ending is important.

ON BEING BAD AT MAKING GAMES
zKevin started out making games in Roblox by messing around with the free models that were available and slowly working toward scripting. However, when quizzed on what made him stick with it, he isn't entirely sure. "I was always bad at making them," he says. "It's always sort of been a domino chain of 'Oh, how do I do this?' situations until eventually I was skilled enough to make a game."

ON STICKING WITH ROBLOX
"I used to think I would switch to a different system but then it kinda hit me what I was doing," he says, of his moment of Roblox realization. "The number of players I was reaching was way beyond anything I could ever imagine on any other platform."

ON THE JOY OF A GOOD ENDING
"The ending of Cleaning Simulator always brings me so much joy," zKevin says. The multiplayer nature of Roblox means that a lot of games are endless, or driven by creating continuous adventures with others. zKevin took a different path for Cleaning Simulator, and was partially influenced by nostalgia: "It's so nice to have a Roblox game with a proper ending, just like the games of my childhood. Kind of like the cherry on the top of video games."

LUMBER TYCOON 2

Settle into life on a lumber yard of your own construction in Lumber Tycoon 2! You'll fell trees, and shape them into logs to sell for better equipment and tools. You'll explore varied lands, drive vehicles, construct machines to automate your work, and steadily build your dream home!

Take timber to the wood drop-off at the side of Wood R Us to earn money! Invest it in a $100 plot of land at the Land Store.

Buy a Basic Hatchet from the Wood R Us shop. Then cut down a nearby oak tree. You can chop the tree into smaller pieces once it's been felled to make it easier to transport.

Buy a Shabby Sawmill and place it on your land. Feed wood into it to make more valuable wood planks.

Upgrade your hatchet and buy a truck that will carry your timber. Keep upgrading your tools and sawmill and in time you'll be building a luxurious house on your plot!

GAME STATS

DEVELOPER:	Defaultio
SUBGENRES:	Tycoon, Crafting
VISITS:	
FAVORITED:	

QUICK TIPS

EARLY BONUS
When you buy your plot of land at the start of the game, take your purchase sign to the drop-off for a very welcome $400! If you ever run out of space, remember you can expand your property at the Land Store.

WOOD WORLD
Explore the world! Visit its many different biomes, try cutting down the unique trees you find in them, and investigate every detail. There are many secrets to find, such as the super-powerful Rukiryaxe tool ...

EFFICIENT MECHS
Make work easier with conveyor belts, buttons, and levers to automate the flow of wood into your truck. You can use components from stores like Link's Logic Shop, found in the tropics biome, to create these machines.

WHEELER DEALER
Trade wood and gear with other players! Barter in chat, then send money on the menu and whitelist them so they can interact with your property. Make sure you trust them and blacklist anyone you don't want on your plot.

DEFAULTIO

Defaultio is a Roblox veteran, having signed up all the way back in 2007. Here he explains how he became a developer even though he never intended to be one, the real challenge of a successful career, and how part of his secret is being the best at keeping secrets!

ON BEING AN ACCIDENTAL DEVELOPER
Despite Lumber Tycoon 2's complexity, Defaultio never had any intention of making games when he first played Roblox. "I just signed up because I liked to build things. Pretty soon I discovered I could use Lua to make even more interesting things, and I just kept making stuff. As Roblox evolved, I also developed from a kid building wacky stuff into a game developer."

ON ROBLOX SUCCESS
"I think that people often underestimate the time that it takes to build games," he says, explaining that famous devs have spent months perfecting the craft. "We put that time in because it's fun and we love what we do, but it's also a ton of work. Making games like Lumber Tycoon 2 demands a lot of talent and knowledge."

ON COMMUNITY FEEDBACK
"I like to collect ideas from the community and I'll work with them," Defaultio says, but it's important to keep secrets about what Lumber Tycoon 2's updates will include. "I always need to keep everyone on their toes. They never know what might be coming."

SKYBOUND 2

Take to the skies in a contraption of your own crafting, scavenge crystals on floating islands, and dogfight with other intrepid adventurers in Skybound 2. Following the success of Skybound, this sequel debuted in 2014 and friends have been battling above the clouds ever since.

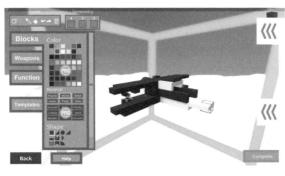

⟨⟨⟨ Customization allows you to choose everything about your ship, from the weapons it uses, down to the texture of each individual block.

⟨⟨⟨ You'll see ships ranging from "small" to "titanic" taking to the skies. Just remember, the bigger they are, the harder they fall!

Skybound 2's islands play host to crystal-strewn plains, which are perfect for engaging in deadly sword battles, while the trees provide enough cover for a tense gunfight. ⟩⟩⟩

C4 can destroy ships, but can also come in handy during melee battles. The blast will knock enemies over, allowing attackers to land a quick hit with a sword or gun.

GAME STATS

DEVELOPER:	Imaginaerum
SUBGENRES:	Crafting, PvP, Exploration
VISITS:	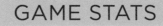
FAVORITED:	

QUICK TIPS

GETTING STARTED
First, either choose one of the three template ships, or create your own flying machine by mixing up dozens of unique blocks. Get familiar with the controls by using the biplane or helicopter first.

LIFESAVER
The most valuable spawn item is the leafblower. If your ship is destroyed, it can help you reach the nearest island safely. Keep an eye on the fuel, though, or you could end up stalling over the dark abyss!

CRYSTAL HOARD
Collect as many crystals as you can. Use them to unlock different ship sizes, which release better weapons and additional blocks that can be combined to make your ship even more unique.

SECRET WEAPON
If you are constantly being shot down by a bigger ship, use the leafblower to board it. Once there, plant C4 and detonate it, then use the leafblower again to jump away. Repeat until the ship is destroyed.

IMAGINAERUM

Skybound 2 was developed by Imaginaerum, who has been a member of the Roblox community since 2009, and started building games shortly after, in 2010. His first hit was Skybound, now known as Skybound Classic, which has been played over 4 million times!

ON BECOMING A DEVELOPER
Think a highly successful developer like Imaginaerum planned this path all along? "I can't think of any one thing or time when I was like 'wow, I really want to be a game developer.' I just played around with Studio until I got good enough to make things I thought sounded fun."

ON PLAYING GAMES
"I loved playing 'build to survive' games when I started on Roblox. My favorite memory is a game where you had to build a boat and sail it across a deadly river. My friends and I built a

massive frigate and reached the end on a single block." The influence of building and survival games are clear to see in the Skybound series.

ON DEVELOPER ENVY
Imaginaerum's love of building has made him a big fan of another top Roblox game. "I think I look up to Lumber Tycoon 2 the most. I love the idea of the physics-based resource collection." Although there are a few things he would have done differently. "If I had made the game I think I would've made it more survival-based with a crafting system and different materials."

KICK OFF

Take to the field in a game of soccer between two titanic teams! Pass, tackle, and shoot your way to victory in a simple and super-fun take on the world's most popular sport that anyone can play. Skill is crucial, but it'll be teamwork that wins the day.

Ensure you celebrate when you score! You'll get points for passing, scoring, and winning matches, which you can spend on new animations and boosts. ⟪

Each game lasts four minutes, beginning at kick-off. Teams are even and each goalie is controlled by the computer. ⟫

Run into the ball to start dribbling it. Hold the action button to run faster, but this will deplete your stamina. ⟫

⟪ When the opposition has possession, slide toward them to tackle them. Don't worry, you can't hurt players or give away fouls.

GAME STATS

STUDIO:	CM Games
SUBGENRES:	Sports
VISITS:	
FAVORITED:	

QUICK TIPS

PASS MASTER
Kick Off is all about good positioning: make sure you and your team use the whole field, finding space away from opposing players so you can run for the goal when the ball is passed to you.

SLIDE RULE
Tackle wisely! You have limited movement once you start to slide, so be sure to aim well. You don't want to be sliding the wrong way as the opposition runs in to score!

SILKY SKILLS
Increase shot power by holding down the button as you kick. You can also perform Trickshots when your Trickshot gauge is full. It's great for smashing the ball into the back of the net.

CALL IT
You can shout out commands to your teammates – PASS, SHOOT, and CROSS. If you all use them well, they'll help to organize the team strategy. If used badly, then it's just a lot of shouting.

LETHAL682

While playing Stickmasterluke's Natural Disaster Survival with his friends in 2014, Lethal682 soon found himself making new friends in the game, which inspired him to begin making games for himself! Here, he explains how he got started, and how easy it is to doubt what you make.

ON LEARNING TO PROGRAM
Lethal682 chose Roblox because he found it welcoming to someone new to making games. "I had no prior knowledge of programming before joining Roblox, but it was easy to learn," he says. "I started off small with learning to code. On the wiki there are many tutorials for all levels of learners. For young people wanting to learn how to program, Roblox is the perfect platform to make their ideas a reality."

ON FINDING PLAYERS
Being easy to make games in Roblox is one thing, but as Lethal682 says, it wouldn't be so great if it was difficult to get people to

play. "There is a huge diverse community on Roblox. No matter your game idea, there will be someone out there who will enjoy it. And with all the tools needed to create a game being free, I had no reason not to give it a go."

ON DOUBT
Kick Off might seem like an obviously appealing game, but Lethal682 didn't feel the same way while he was making it. "Kick Off was in development for over a year!" he says. "It was a project that I kept putting off because I doubted its potential. I was amazed by the positive response after I released Kick Off and regretted not working on it sooner."

DESIGN IT!

Command the catwalk in Design It!, a fashion competition in which players assemble the best outfits to fit a theme and then vote for the winner. You only get a certain budget to work with, though, so choose your garb wisely, think stylishly, and impress fellow contestants with your creativity!

Each round starts with a theme. It could be a color, like pink, or a topic like "western" or "sports." You have five minutes to create the perfect outfit from the available clothes, faces, and accessories.

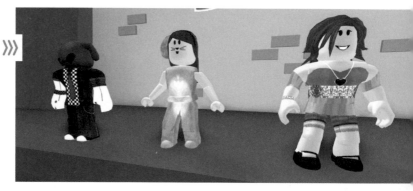

When the design phase ends, the show starts. You can't see usernames, so vote for the costume you like best.

As you play rounds and get podium finishes for your costumes, you'll find your budget increases, so you can add more and more flamboyant gear to your ensemble.

GAME STATS

DEVELOPER:	tktech
SUBGENRES:	Town and City, Fashion, PvP
VISITS:	
FAVORITED:	

QUICK TIPS

SNEAK PEEK
Finish your design early and check the lobby to get a crafty look at how your rivals interpreted the theme. You can then go back to tweak your creation using your new inspiration!

BIG REVEAL
Alternatively, if you've designed a masterpiece outfit, you can wait until the last minute to complete your design, giving your rivals no opportunity to copy your finest work.

WORD SEARCH
The search tool is a secret weapon! Think of words related to the theme and see if searching them yields any good stuff. You'll be surprised how often a great item appears in the results.

CATWALK
Don't forget to use emotes to attract attention to yourself on the stage. Remember the key to standing out is to be surprising or funny, or by putting a clever spin on a theme.

TKTECH

tktech has been making games in Roblox since he first joined in 2010, attracted by the chance to make places to play with his friends. Read on to learn about how the inspirational qualities of egg hunts and the launch of Design It! was just the beginning of the journey!

ON LEARNING NEW SKILLS
"Despite my skillset as a developer growing exponentially, I can still find ways to challenge myself on a daily basis to create bigger and better products, all within the Roblox framework." And they're not only useful in Roblox itself. "You can take them into the real world, no matter where you start from."

ON EGG HUNTS
"My fondest memory of playing Roblox games is participating in the Roblox holiday events," tktech says. He joined Roblox just before the second Egg Hunt of 2010 was due to begin. His unerring curiosity became motivation to pick up Roblox. "It was a super-fun introduction to Roblox. I loved the fact that I could hunt for eggs in any place, including my own, and that's one of the reasons I started looking at Roblox Studio. I wanted to have a game in which people wanted to hunt for eggs."

ON LAUNCHING FAST
Believe it or not, the first release of Design It! took only seven days to make! But really, that was just the start of the project for tktech. "Since hitting the number one spot on the front page just hours after beta release, I've put a countless amount of work into making the game exponentially better than the first release."

CLONE TYCOON 2

Clone yourself to build an army and defeat all challengers! Earn money to upgrade their abilities, give them fearsome weapons, and dress them in the best outfits. Remember, while you're improving your clones, your opponents' clones are becoming more powerful too.

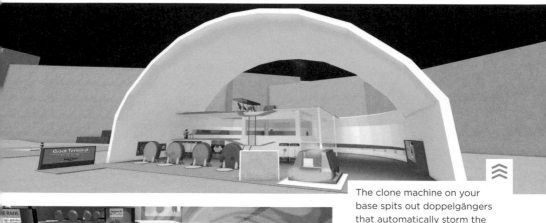

The clone machine on your base spits out doppelgängers that automatically storm the battlefield and fight with other players' clones to earn money.

Once you've upgraded your base enough, you'll be able to edit clone machines to add special effects on every clone they produce. You can also upgrade your clones' durability and speed.

Your base can be upgraded with dozens of different options, including research labs, pet enclosures, and weapon racks, as well as multiple rooms and floors to hold all your scientific developments.

GAME STATS

DEVELOPER:	Ultraw
SUBGENRES:	Sci-Fi, Tycoon, Fighting
VISITS:	
FAVORITED:	

QUICK TIPS

CLONE CONVOY
Eventually you'll unlock vehicles, which you can load with clones. You can set the clones down at strategic points to coordinate attacks on opposing bases and max out your kill count.

FOR SCIENCE
Earn more money by building the research labs. Upgrade them so your clones earn more money per kill. They can also be upgraded to earn gems that can be used to buy pets!

DOPPELGÄNGER
Get involved in the battles yourself by upgrading your base with a series of deadly weapons. You'll need to turn on Battle Mode from the options on the left to be able to fight the clones.

COSTUME PARTY
Besides upgrading your clones' stats and special abilities, you can customize their look with the morph buttons. Now you can send out armies of mechs or even penguins to fight for your cause!

ULTRAW

Ultraw has been playing Roblox since 2010 and was inspired to create the original Clone Tycoon when he found himself disappointed with another game promising fighting clones. He began making his own version of the concept to prevent others from suffering the same fate.

ON BECOMING A GAME DEVELOPER

Ultraw believes that Roblox is the perfect starting place for anyone who wants to get into making games. He should know – it's where he started out too! "Over the last four years, I have progressed from a beginner to a great scripter. It was made a lot easier by the tools and tutorials that Roblox offers."

ON GETTING NEW IDEAS

The Roblox community is a constant source of ideas for many games, and Ultraw explains that community feedback accounts for much of his inspiration. "I receive many messages that contain amazing ideas that make it into

my games." But he warns against relying on it too much, because some of them can be a little crazy. "As a developer you have to have a vision for your game, and you can allow the community to take it in the right direction, but not take your game completely off course."

ON HIS FAVORITE ROBLOX MEMORIES

One of Ultraw's fondest memories on Roblox is playing badge-hunting games for endless hours with his friends. "My favorite one was Find the Domos. Looking back on them now, they were very simple games, but I remember being captivated by them as I had to discover all the map's secrets!"

ASSASSIN!

Your mission in this fast-paced deathmatch is to assassinate your target among the seven other players. The catch, however, is that one of them is your own assassin! In this game of cat and mouse you'll need to use your wits as well as your knife. Will you be the last player standing?

Each round, you and seven other players spawn at random around one of Assassin!'s maps. Your target is displayed at the top of the screen.

You can only kill your target or the player trying to hunt you. If you hit another player you won't be able to use your knife for a few seconds!

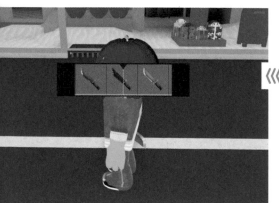

You'll earn coins for playing and taking out targets. Spend them on opening cases to get random knives, snazzy visual effects, and pets to go into battle with.

GAME STATS

DEVELOPER:	prisman
SUBGENRES:	Fighting, Mystery
VISITS:	▮
FAVORITED:	▮

QUICK TIPS

MUG SHOT

Memorize a target's portrait so you know what to look for in the crowd. Recognizing their clothes from across the level instead of getting close to see their name makes a big difference.

WATCH YOUR SIX

If a player seems to be following you, there's a chance you're their target. Turning to face your potential attacker is better than running away, and you'll get XP and coins for taking them down.

START RIGHT

Use the few seconds at the start of the match when you can't use your knife to scout out the level. If you can find your target before they can act, you could get a jump on them.

NEAR OR FAR

Learning to throw your knife at moving targets is tricky as you have to hold the button, so save this for slower targets. Often it's more effective to move in and swing your knife for a melee kill.

PRISMAN

The developer of Assassin!, prisman, has been a player on Roblox since 2009 and started to make games in 2011. Here he explains how to be better at his game, how he goes about starting new development projects, and what he thinks is so special about the Roblox community.

ON ASSASSIN!'S BEST FEATURE

prisman is most proud of Assassin!'s social aspect, in which players meet up to trade items, form clans, and host their own tournaments. "When a game's community can take the game and make what they want out of it, you have something special." It goes so far that almost all Assassin!'s new updates are based on asking the community what it wants!

ON DESIGNING GAMES

"Definitely start with the gameplay mechanics," he advises, because it's the design that keeps players coming back to play, not the quality of the graphics or the characters. "For Assassin! it was the 'hunt your target' system, and then, once I have a solid gameplay mechanic that I wish to expand upon, I'll move on to the theme, genre, or story."

ON STAYING MOTIVATED

His favorite aspect of being part of the Roblox community is its creative atmosphere. "You can create almost anything you can imagine on Roblox if you put the time and effort into it, and easily put your creations out into the world where people can play with them," he says. "Seeing the crazy, super unique projects that other developers take on motivates me to keep creating on a daily basis."

SWORDBURST ONLINE

Explore a fantasy world and battle fearsome beasts in Swordburst Online. You'll craft new gear and find legendary weapons, raising your power enough to face epic bosses that hold the keys to progressing deeper into this dangerous land.

◀◀◀ You start in Vagrant's Keep, almost ready to do battle. Equip your sword and armor in the inventory and teleport to Agnaroth Plains from the statue.

◀◀◀ Wandering the plains are boars and wolves. Starter players can tackle a boar. Your health regenerates, so wait awhile to recover before tackling another.

◀◀◀ For each kill you'll get experience, money, and materials. Craft in Vagrant's Keep by choosing five items that match your crafting level.

◀◀◀ Team up with other players to take on the first area's boss before entering the maze in the tower. If you can get through and kill the Kobold King, you'll access the next floor!

GAME STATS

DEVELOPER:	AbstractAlex
SUBGENRES:	RPG, Fighting
VISITS:	
FAVORITED:	

QUICK TIPS

LOOT DROP

Enemies drop items when they die, some of which are rare. For example, The Dire Wolf of Agnaroth Plains drops a deadly sword known as the Skyduster, but beware, this lupine is guarded by more fearsome wolves.

KING SLAYER

To progress beyond the Agnaroth Plains you'll need to face the Kobold King and do at least 20% of the damage to kill him without dying. He drops the Justifier, a two-handed sword that boosts both defense and attack!

SHOPPING TRIP

You start with an iron sword but you can buy other weapons in the beginner shop, like a shield or spear. Each weapon has benefits: the shield raises defense and health regeneration, while the spear has greater attack.

WEAPON SMITH

The items you craft depend on the level of ore you use. Steel weapons can be crafted with Ivory Ore from boars. Once your crafting reaches level five, you can start using Wind Ore to create even more powerful weapons.

ABSTRACTALEX

There are all kinds of game developers around Roblox, some working alone, some with teams. AbstractAlex is one of the devs who loves to work with others. Here he explains how he got into game development and what happened when he took an internship at Roblox HQ!

ON GETTING INTO CREATING

"After school, my friends and I would always head home and play MMORPGs together," he remembers. "I was definitely more interested than most of my friends so I started to learn how to make them. I tried various tools and eventually stumbled upon Roblox because it was the easiest. I was able to learn code and play games at the same time."

ON HIS ROBLOX INTERNSHIP

In 2015, AbstractAlex took a Roblox internship, during which he got to work from their HQ along with other top developers. "Defaultio made a spaceship simulator. Each player's computer acted as a different terminal on the spaceship, controlling things like weapons, power, and steering, and we had a projector displaying the actual ship. We had two teams of four players battling each other. It was a unique experience!"

ON A CRAZY SECRET BEHIND ROBLOX

"Houses have no furniture when nobody is inside of them," he says. "But you never see this because if you're looking, it means you're inside the house so it will have furniture!"

ACHIEVEMENT CHECKLIST

Now that you're an adventure game aficionado, it's time to take things to the next level. Below is a list of the trickiest challenges these games have to offer and how to get your hands on them. Can you complete them all and become an adventurer of legend?

NOMAD
APOCALYPSE RISING

Only the hardiest players have what it takes to earn this achievement, which requires 750 zombie kills and 30 days of survival. Sounds simple, but it doesn't account for other survivors trying to hunt you down.

TOP GUN
JAILBREAK

Channel your inner action hero to earn this badge, by shooting down a helicopter while riding in a vehicle. Make sure you've got a powerful weapon and are riding shotgun to take down a chopper.

CLOSE CALL
NATURAL DISASTER SURVIVAL

Being a skilled survivor isn't a necessity to claim this award. Instead, you need to take damage so you're within an inch of dying, under 10 HP to be precise, and still survive the current disaster. It's a fine line to tread ...

BIG BANG THEORY
INNOVATION LABS

To attain this badge, all you need to do is create a new universe. Head to the core control, hit three buttons on the left of the console, then align the Calibrate Receiver to the notches. Hit the main panel button, then cross the bridge.

DEAD-VELOPER
SKYBOUND 2

What better way to thank a developer for their hard work than by taking them down in their own game? Kill either Imaginaerum, Injanity, AlexxTC, or Alexej200 in the game to surpass their pirating skills and grab this badge.

PLUNDERER
TRADELANDS
This achievement is reserved for only the most brazen of buccaneers. Become a feared pirate thief and smuggle a unit of cargo from someone else's ship, then sell it while at least 10 other seafarers are playing.

DISCOVER: SKY ISLAND
TEMPLE OF MEMORIES
Mastering the art of meditation is a piece of cake compared to reaching the floating Sky Island in Temple of Memories. If you can find this hidden location, you'll achieve this badge — as well as enlightenment!

SECRET BADGE
HEROES OF ROBLOXIA
After saving Robloxia by taking down the devious Darkmatter, there's just one secret left to find. Explore all corners of the hero tower to discover it, and land this mysterious achievement.

GREEN FLOWER
WOLVES' LIFE 2
Search high and low to find the rarest of flowers and unlock this badge. As well as giving you a significant sense of achievement, your wolf will also now leave a sparkly green trail behind him.

AIRBORNE ALIEN
ZOMBIE RUSH
Annihilating thousands of zombies is all well and good, but you can't call yourself a true zombie hunter until you've touched the UFO on the farm map. You're one leap away from an impressive badge to add to your collection.

DESTROYED SHIP
GALAXY
This one is very simple – just destroy another ship in a space battle, which you were going to do anyway! The only caveat is that it needs to be a ship that your enemy has paid to create, so not just a starter Wasp ship.

FLIGHT
SHARD SEEKERS

Shrug off the shackles of land-based travel by transforming into a flying character or pet and taking to the skies. Going by air rather than land will net you the rarest badge in Shard Seekers.

LEGENDARY ORANGE GOAT BADGE
WHATEVER FLOATS YOUR BOAT

This unusually named badge has absolutely nothing to do with goats. Rather, it's about hitting level 50 and then letting five of your ships sink completely. Makes sense, doesn't it?

ABOMINATION!
PINEWOOD COMPUTER CORE

Descend to the darkest depths of the secret facility to discover the glowing green figures that lurk beneath and unlock this badge. They don't look too healthy so you probably shouldn't get too close …

EVOLVED
MINER'S HAVEN

This badge could take a while. First you'll need to go through rebirth to attain reborn items, then fuse them together to create an evolved reborn item. Your mine's productivity will be hugely increased as a reward!

IMPRESSIVE AGILITY
FLOOD ESCAPE

You'll need skill and consistency to collect this badge, but the rules are pretty simple. You just need to win five times on hard mode in a single game session. Much easier said than done, however!

GAVIN'S SECRET
THE NORMAL ELEVATOR

Enter a tense new dimension of the floor-crawler by using Gavin's code on the keypad in the lobby (Hint: it contains these numbers: 9, 2, 7, and 3). Then ride the elevator to hear Gavin's story, and collect this cool badge.

10 TRUCKS
MINING INC!
Another fairly self-explanatory achievement to accomplish. Enhance your burgeoning mining empire with a fleet of at least ten trucks to make work in the dark mines easy, and get a brand-new badge in the process.

THE ULTIMATE DUNK
CLEANING SIMULATOR
Show off your sparkling sports skills to achieve this badge. First, find a basketball and make your way to the roof of the BRIBBLECO building, then lob it off the roof and into the hoop down below. Swish!

1000 GOALS
KICK OFF
Lace up your shooting boots and get ready to hammer home some hat tricks. Your task here is to rack up a total of 1000 goals – obviously. It doesn't matter how many games it takes, so you can still pass now and then.

COLORFUL DESIGNER
DESIGN IT!
Designing a cool outfit is one thing, but there are some things only money can buy. Get your hands on all the purchasable effects in the game to take your outfit and your badge collection to the next level.

PLANET I
CLONE TYCOON 2
Take your clones to the stratosphere by herding them to a brand-new planet. Talk to the female astronaut to reach the new world, then defeat the evil Eye Lord to land this achievement.

COMPETITIVE TOP 100
ASSASSIN!
This one requires equal parts luck and skill. You'll need to be one of the 100 best players at the end of an in-game season to achieve this, which is no easy feat. There's even a badge for reaching the top 10 for elite adventurers.

GOODBYE!

AHOY THERE, ME HEARTY!

You've navigated all the way here on your own, have ye? You must be the mysterious Robloxian who's been besting adventures across the land. The high winds have brought me tales of your journeys by sea and by sky, and shiver me timbers, they're not bad for a landlubber.

But know this, matey, the adventures across the land of Robloxia are never-ending. The odysseys that ye maneuvered to reach this waypoint are but the tip of a colossal iceberg.

One piece of advice, though I suspect you already know it – never rest on your booty for too long, because new adventures are springing up every day. Right now there are enough expeditions in Robloxia to fill a thousand dusty tomes to bursting, which is not to say ye've not done well thus far. Just know that your true adventure has only just begun.

EZEBEL: THE PIRATE QUEEN

A GUIDE TO SOCIALIZING ONLINE WITH ROBLOX

YOUNGER FANS' GUIDE TO ROBLOX

Roblox might be your first experience of digital socializing, so here are a few simple rules to help you stay safe and keep the internet a great place to spend time.

- Never give out your real name – don't use it as your username.

- Never give out any of your personal details.
- Never tell anybody which school you go to or how old you are.
- Never tell anybody your password except a parent or guardian.
- Always tell a parent or guardian if something is worrying you.

PARENTS' GUIDE TO ROBLOX

Roblox has security and privacy settings that enable you to monitor and limit your child's access to the social features on Roblox, or turn them off completely. You can also limit the range of games your child can access, view their activity histories, and report inappropriate activity on the site.

To restrict your child from playing, chatting, and messaging with others on Roblox, log in to your child's account and click on the **gear icon** in the upper right-hand corner and select **Settings**. From here you can access the **Security** and **Privacy** menus:

- Users register for Roblox with their date of birth. It's important for children to enter the correct date because Roblox has default security and privacy settings that vary based on a player's age – this can be checked and changed in **Settings**.

- To review and restrict your child's social settings go to **Settings** and select **Privacy**. Review the options under **Contact Settings** and **Other Settings**. Select **No one** or **Everyone.** Note: players age 13 and older have additional options.

- To control the safety features that are implemented on your child's account, you'll need to set up a 4-digit PIN. This will lock all of the settings, only enabling changes once the PIN is entered. To enable an Account PIN, go to the **Settings** page, select **Security**, and turn **Account PIN** to **ON**.

To help monitor your child's account, you can view the history for certain activities:

- To view your child's private message history, choose **Messages** from the menu bar down the left-hand side of the main screen. If the menu bar isn't visible, click on the list icon in the left-hand corner.

- To view your child's chat history, open the **Chat & Party** window, located bottom-right. You can then click on any of the listed users to open a window with the chat history.

- To view your child's online friends and followers, choose **Friends** from the menu bar down the left-hand side of the main screen.

- To view your child's creations choose **Develop** from the tabs running along the top of the main screen.

- To view any virtual items purchased and any trade history, choose **Trade** from the menu bar then go to **My Transactions**.

While the imagery on Roblox has a largely blocky, digitized look, parents should be aware that some of the user-generated games may include themes or imagery that may be too intense for young or sensitive players:

- You can limit your child's account to display only a restricted list of available games to play. Go to **Settings**, select **Security**, and turn on **Account Restrictions**.

Roblox players of all ages have their posts and chats filtered to prevent personal information being shared, but no filter is foolproof. Roblox asks users and parents to report any inappropriate activity. Check your child's account and look to see if they have friends they do not know. Talk to your child about what to report (including bullying, inappropriate behavior or messages, scams and other game violations):

- To report concerning behavior on Roblox, use the **Report Abuse** links located on game, group, and user pages and in the **Report** tab of every game menu.

- To block another player during a game session, find the user on the leaderboard/player list at the upper-right of the game screen. (If the leaderboard/player list isn't there, open it by clicking on your username in the upper-right corner.) From here, click on the player and select **Block User**.

For further information, Roblox has created a parents' guide to the website, which can be accessed at https://corp.roblox.com/parents